SEARCHING
THE SCRIPTURES

SEARCHING
THE SCRIPTURES

*Bringing Power to Your Personal
and Family Study*

GENE R. COOK

DESERET BOOK COMPANY · SALT LAKE CITY, UTAH

*To all those who truly cherish the words of the Lord
and are doing their best to incorporate them
into their daily living*

Library of Congress Cataloging-in-Publication Data

Cook, Gene R.
  Searching the Scriptures / by Gene R. Cook.
    p.   cm.
  Includes index.
  ISBN 1-57345-247-5 (hardcover)
  1. Mormon Church—Sacred books—Study and teaching. 2. Church of
Jesus Christ of Latter-day Saints—Doctrines—Study and teaching.
I. Title.
  BX8622.C66   1997
  289.3'2—dc21   97-13603
                                                                CIP

Printed in the United States of America   72082

10 9   8   7   6   5   4   3   2   1

CONTENTS

PART 3

FAMILY STUDY:
BLESSING YOUR FAMILY WITH THE WORD OF THE LORD

ACKNOWLEDGMENTS

I am indebted to the Spirit of the Lord through the years for teaching me and causing me to truly love the words of the Lord. I also feel a great debt of gratitude to those who have taught me to highly esteem the holy scriptures, including my family, many teachers, friends, and others.

Special thanks goes particularly to Sister Stephanie Colquitt, one of my former secretaries, for her assistance in typing up some of the key materials that were used in a talk on the scriptures, which later produced the outline and basis for this book.

Brother Jay A. Parry provided valued assistance in the editing and preparation of the manuscript for printing. He is an excellent editor who is able to take ideas and present them in a simple, inspired fashion to benefit the reader.

It is hoped that the material in this book might inspire the reader to truly search the holy scriptures more diligently. It is also my desire that the reader may learn better how to continually hear the voice of the Lord and thereby be able to resolve life's daily challenges.

Lastly, I would like to say that this book is not in any way an official publication of The Church of Jesus Christ of Latter-day Saints. Any shortcomings, omissions, or deficiencies are clearly mine as the one solely responsible for the material in this book.

WHY READ THIS BOOK

"O that I were an angel," Alma exclaimed, ". . . that I might go forth and speak with . . . a voice to shake the earth." He would proclaim repentance, he said, inviting "every soul" to "come unto our God, that there might not be more sorrow upon all the face of the earth." (Alma 29:1–2.)

Alma's desires are my desires—and I know they're shared by many others as well.

O that I were an angel, that I might proclaim the sweetness and wonder of God's word, that all the people of the whole world might come to the blessing of "feasting upon the word of Christ" as it is found in the scriptures. (2 Ne. 31:20.)

O that I were an angel, that I could help people learn how to search the scriptures more diligently—and to motivate them to search daily.

O that I were an angel, that I could convince families everywhere to discover the power of family scripture reading.

I suspect it's impossible for anyone to fully convey his feeling for the true value and importance of the scriptures. I fear that all of us treat them lightly, not giving them the time, attention, or thought they deserve. But I also believe that if we have a deeper understanding of what the scriptures really are, it will motivate us to view them differently, to treat them differently, and to truly seek, by the Spirit of the Lord, to understand what the Lord is saying to us through them.

I love the words of the hymn that says, "As I search the holy scriptures. . . ." The standard works are not just *scriptures;* they are *holy.* I believe they ought to be handled in a holy way. They ought to be thought of in a holy way. They are the very words of God.

> As I search the holy scriptures,
> Loving Father of mankind,
> May my heart be blessed with wisdom,
> And may knowledge fill my mind.

When you read the scriptures with the Spirit, you do indeed feel knowledge fill your mind.

> As I search the holy scriptures,
> Touch my spirit, Lord, I pray.
> May life's mysteries be unfolded
> As I study day by day.

Through the scriptures the Lord can bless us—not just month by month or week by week, but day by day.

> As I search the holy scriptures,
> May thy mercy be revealed.
> Soothe my troubled heart and spirit;
> May my unseen wounds be healed.

Isn't that your experience when you read the scriptures? I know it is mine. They truly do soothe the troubled heart and spirit. If we will read the word of the Lord with the Spirit of the Lord, what peace they can bring to us. And how many "unseen wounds" do they heal in us? I'm confident that your experience has been like mine: as I read and ponder and pray, I feel the Lord speak to me and truly heal the wounds hidden within my heart.

WHY READ THIS BOOK

As I search the holy scriptures,
Help me ponder and obey.
In thy word is life eternal;
May thy light show me the way.
(*Hymns* [Salt Lake City: The Church
of Jesus Christ of Latter-day Saints,
1985], 277.)

To ponder and to obey are two key principles of searching the scriptures—we'll talk in some detail about both in this book. As we ponder and obey the scriptures, they'll show us the way to walk in this life. And they'll show us the way back home. After all, that's ultimately what they were given for—to help us learn how to return home, once again, to our Heavenly Father.

How Can This Book Help You?

It is my hope that this book will both motivate you and serve as a practical guide as you search the scriptures more diligently. In the first section of the book, about the power and blessing of the Lord's word, we focus on the purpose and importance of the scriptures—not only for the Church, but also for each of us individually.

One of the most valuable purposes of the scriptures is to serve as a tool to help us hear the voice of the Lord. But that blessing doesn't come through casual effort. Instead, we need to search the scriptures diligently: pondering and questioning, marking and cross-referencing, and seeking understanding of how they apply to our lives. Then we need to obey what we understand. The second section of the book seeks to explore how we can effectively do those things.

The third section is designed to be a blessing to families. Again, I hope it will serve to motivate and be a practical aid to families as they seek to learn better how to search the scriptures together. Taking cues from the experience of my own family, as well as others, I offer suggestions on how to organize for family study, how to invite and maintain the Spirit of the Lord in your family reading time, and how to use the scriptures as a way to bless each member of your family.

As you read the pages of this book, I invite you to pray for the guidance of the Spirit of the Lord. Ask the Lord to open your heart and mind so you can receive truth and be blessed by it. If you will do that with an honest heart, I promise you that the Lord will bless you and help you to grow in your understanding and appreciation of these great books, which are nothing less than a record of the words of God revealed to his children on the earth.

THE PURPOSE OF THE SCRIPTURES

THE POWER AND BLESSING OF THE LORD'S WORD

CHAPTER 1

WORTH ANY
SACRIFICE

What is the power of the scriptures? How important are they? Here is a fascinating true story that will give us some clues.

In 1910 a young Italian preacher in New York City, named Don Vincenzo di Francesca, found a book on top of a barrel of ashes. "Curious, I picked up the book and knocked it against the side of the barrel to shake the ashes from its pages," he wrote.

THE BOOK WITHOUT A COVER

As I stood there with the book in my hands, the fury of the wind turned the pages, and one by one, the names Nephi, Mosiah, Alma, Moroni, and Isaiah appeared before my eyes. Since the cold wind was bitter, I hurriedly wrapped the soiled book in a newspaper and continued my journey. . . .

Back in my room I carefully turned the torn pages. . . . What could be the name of the church that taught such doctrine in words so easily understood? The cover of the book and the title page were missing. I read the declaration of witnesses in the opening pages and was strongly impressed by the strength of their testimonies, but there was no other clue to the book's identity.

I purchased some alcohol and cotton from the

drugstore beneath my lodgings and began cleaning the soiled pages. Then for several hours I read what was written in the book. When I had read chapter ten of the book of Moroni, I locked the door of my room; and with the book held in my hands, I knelt down and asked God, the Eternal Father, in the name of his Son Jesus Christ, to tell me if the book was of God. As I prayed, I felt my body becoming cold. Then my heart began to pound, and a feeling of warmth and gladness came over me and filled me with such joy that I cannot find words to express. I knew that the words of the book came from God.

I continued my services in the parish, but my preaching was tinged with the new words I had found in the book. The members of my congregation were so interested in my words that they became dissatisfied with the sermons of my colleagues, and they asked them why they did not preach the sweet arguments of Don Vincenzo. This was the beginning of troubles for me. When members began leaving the chapel during the sermons of my colleagues and remained when I occupied the pulpit, my colleagues became angry with me.

"I COULD NOT DENY THE WORDS OF THE BOOK"

Don Vincenzo eventually was called before a "committee of censure" for disciplinary action. They instructed him to burn the book, saying it was of the devil. Vincenzo replied that the book was the word of God.

"I declared that if I were to burn the book, I would displease God. I would rather go out of the congregation of the church than offend him."

The council dropped the matter until 1914, when he was again instructed to burn the book.

"In reply, I stated I could not deny the words of the book

nor would I burn it, since in doing so I would offend God. I said I looked forward with joy to the time when the church to which the book belonged would be made known to me and I would become a part of it."

The council responded by stripping him of his position as pastor of the church. Three weeks later he was excommunicated.

In 1914 he was drafted into the Italian army and saw action in Europe during World War I. "Remembering the lessons of the book I had read, I related to some of the men in my company the story of the people of Ammon—how they refused to shed the blood of their brothers and buried their arms rather than be guilty of so great crimes. The chaplain reported me to the colonel. . . . I received as punishment a ten-day sentence on bread and water, with the order that I was to speak no more of the book and its stories."

After the war Vincenzo was readmitted to his church in New York and was sent by them on a mission to New Zealand and Australia. While teaching the people, he continued to share truths from the Book of Mormon. His companion "reported me to the synod, and . . . I was cut off from the church forever. Soon after, I returned to Italy."

"AT LONG LAST I LEARNED"

In 1930 he accidentally happened on the entry *Mormon* in a French dictionary. He recognized the name *Mormon* from his book and read the entry carefully. It said that a Mormon Church had been established in 1830 and that this church operated a university at Provo, Utah. It was the first clue he had of where the book without a cover might have come from.

He wrote a letter to the president of the university, which later brought correspondence from President Heber J. Grant and Elder John A. Widtsoe (who was president of the European

Mission). From these brethren Vincenzo received a Book of Mormon in Italian and a pamphlet telling the story of Joseph Smith and the gold plates.

"At long last I had learned the rest of the story begun so long ago when, guided by the hand of God, I found the torn book lying on top of a barrel of ashes on a street in New York City."

Vincenzo sought baptism, but missionaries were unable to reach him because of war in Sicily and later in Europe. For the next thirteen years he had no contact with the Church, but he remained faithful to its teachings—and he continued to share his understandings from the scriptures with others.

Finally, in 1951, he was baptized; as far as we know, it was the first baptism in Sicily. Five years later he was able to receive his endowments in the Swiss Temple.

"At last, to be in the presence of my Heavenly Father!" he wrote. "I felt I had now proved faithful in my second estate, after having searched for and found the true Church by means of an unknown book that I found so many years ago, lying on an open barrel of ashes in the city of New York."

Don Vincenzo di Francesca died in 1966 in Italy, in the province of his birth. (For the full account of his experience, see *Improvement Era*, May 1968, 4–7.)

God's Precious Gifts

I am grateful for this account because it shows a man who was willing to sacrifice everything for the word of God. Brother Vincenzo was willing to sacrifice his employment as a preacher, his membership in his church, and his reputation among his fellowman to stay true to what he had learned in the scriptures.

The scriptures can have such a powerful influence on us that they are worth such sacrifice. Alma and his brethren found that "the preaching of the word had a great tendency to lead the

people to do that which was just—yea, it had had more powerful effect upon the minds of the people than the sword, or anything else, which had happened unto them—therefore Alma
thought it was expedient that they should try the virtue of the
word of God." (Alma 31:5.)

The written word of God—the scriptures—is one of the
greatest blessings the Lord has given us. Until we recognize that
fact, I am afraid we will hold them lightly. Conversely, if we
recognize their supreme importance in our lives—even standing in awe of these precious gifts—we then will treat them with
more respect and greater attention. And, in turn, we will receive
much greater benefits from them.

COST OF PRESERVING SCRIPTURES

How much are *we* willing to sacrifice to give the scriptures a
prominent place in our lives? How important are these things
to *us?*

Some of the best blood that has ever been shed upon the
earth has come from martyrs who sought to preserve and protect the holy word of the Lord. These men felt the scriptures
were so important that they were willing to give their lives for
them. Others, though spared a martyr's death, gave their for-
tunes and sometimes their freedom for the great privilege of
sharing God's word.

John Wycliffe, for example, sought in the 1300s to create an
English translation of the Bible for his countrymen to read. (At
that time, Bibles were translated into Latin, which most people
could not read.) For his desires he was fired from his position
at Oxford and shunned by many friends and associates. One of
his assistants was excommunicated from his church and spent
the next five years in prison or in exile. Wycliffe died soon after
he completed his work. Because of official opposition to his

work with the Bible, his body was later dug up and his bones were burned to ashes, which were then scattered in a river.

In the 1520s and 1530s, after the printing press had been invented, William Tyndale sought to provide a printed version of the English Bible. To escape capture and punishment, he had to travel from city to city in Europe under assumed names. The printing of the Bible had to be done in secret, and the copies could only be smuggled into England. In 1535, in Antwerp, he was betrayed by a friend, captured, and imprisoned. He suffered in a damp dungeon for sixteen months, leaving only for his trial and subsequent execution. He was tied to a stake, strangled, and burned. Refusing to recant, his dying words were, "Lord, open the King of England's eyes."

Others also suffered, and many were put to death just for reading or possessing the forbidden Bibles.

PROTECTING THE BOOK OF MORMON

The Book of Mormon also came at great cost, not only to those who so painstakingly melted ore and created plates on which to record, but also to Joseph Smith and those who sought to help him protect those plates.

Joseph Smith said:

> The . . . heavenly messenger delivered them [the plates] up to me with this charge: that I should be responsible for them; that if I should let them go carelessly, or through any neglect of mine, I should be cut off; but that if I would use all my endeavors to preserve them, until he, the messenger, should call for them, they should be protected.
>
> I soon found out the reason why I had received such strict charges to keep them safe, and why it was that the messenger had said that when I had done what was required at my hand, he would call for them. For no

sooner was it known that I had them, than the most strenuous exertions were used to get them from me. Every stratagem that could be invented was resorted to for that purpose. The persecution became more bitter and severe than before, and multitudes were on the alert continually to get them from me if possible. But by the wisdom of God, they remained safe in my hands, until I had accomplished by them what was required at my hand. (JS-H 1:59–60.)

On the day Joseph Smith actually received the plates from Moroni, he wrapped them in his linen frock and started to carry them home. His mother, Lucy Mack Smith, writes:

After proceeding a short distance, he thought it would be more safe to leave the road and go through the woods. Traveling some distance after he left the road, he came to a large windfall, and as he was jumping over a log, a man sprang up from behind it, and gave him a heavy blow with a gun. Joseph turned around and knocked him down, then ran at the top of his speed. About half a mile further he was attacked again in the same manner as before; he knocked this man down in like manner as the former, and ran on again; and before he reached home he was assaulted the third time. (*Biographical Sketches of Joseph Smith, the Prophet and his Progenitors for Many Generations* [Liverpool: published for Orson Pratt and S. W. Richards, 1853], 104–5.)

When he finally reached the house, he was "speechless from fright and the fatigue of running." (Ibid.)

Joseph's troubles did not end there, of course. He writes: "As soon as news of this discovery [of the gold plates] was made known, false reports, misrepresentation and slander flew, as on the wings of the wind, in every direction; the house was frequently beset by mobs and evil designing persons. Several times I was shot at, and very narrowly escaped, and every device was made use of to get the plates away from me." (Joseph Smith, *History of the Church of Jesus Christ of Latter-day Saints*, ed. B. H. Roberts, 7 vols. [Salt Lake City: The Church of Jesus Christ of Latter-day Saints, 1902–1923], 4:538.)

It was the Lord's plan in the ancient Americas that the plates "should be kept and handed down from one generation to another, and be kept and preserved by the hand of the Lord until they should go forth unto every nation." In doing so, he would "show forth his power unto future generations," namely those of us in this generation. (Alma 37:4, 14.)

Truly a tremendous effort has been made to bring these scriptures to the latter days, to where we stand today. They ought to be held in a sacred way. If they are, and if we can learn how to use them, they will change lives—our own and those we influence.

I love these admonitions from the Lord:

> These words are given unto you, and they are pure before me; wherefore, beware how you hold them, for they are to be answered upon your souls in the day of judgment. (D&C 41:12.)

> These sayings are true and faithful; wherefore, transgress them not, neither take therefrom. (D&C 68:34.)

What a great witness from the Lord himself about the exactness of his word. It causes me to stand in awe, in deep humility, when I think of the greatness of the gift he has given me.

TESTIMONIES OF OTHERS

The Church of Jesus Christ of Latter-day Saints is filled with people who love the scriptures as I do, people who have a deep sense of the value of these volumes. In one of the stakes of Zion, for instance, the stake president challenged his people to read the Book of Mormon before the next stake conference—and they responded with faith and commitment. Here are some of their testimonies of how the scriptures helped to change and bless their lives:

"A Glorious Time"

Our stake president challenged us to read or reread the Book of Mormon prior to our next stake conference. While I had read the Book of Mormon several times before, and had studied it in high school seminary, at Ricks College, and in institute sessions, my new husband had not. He was intrigued by the challenge and thought we should accept it.

My husband is not a member of the Church.

Although we have not yet completed the book, we have been studying each morning for at least thirty minutes when our schedules allow. Often we find more of that time is spent in discussion than in actual reading.

This is the first time in my life that I have gleaned so much from this book, despite all the past years of reading. . . . It has also turned out to be a glorious time for my husband and me to draw closer to each other.

Thank you for helping us to find this added light in our lives!

"I Knew from the First Words"

Rereading the Book of Mormon has been a wonderful reunion, getting reacquainted with my brethren and friends who paved the way on this continent before me.

The first time I read the Book of Mormon was two years before I joined the Church. I was a young mother of two little ones, and my marriage was on the verge of ending. I prayed for the help and strength to hold my little family together and to find the inner peace I so desperately needed. It was then that the Book of Mormon stood out on our bookshelf as if it was illuminated. (The missionaries had left it at our home two years earlier.) I took it down and read the great and comforting words contained therein. I knew from the first words that what I was reading was true. Beginning at that point I made the necessary changes and preparations, so that almost two years later when missionaries again came to my door I was ready for baptism.

My life presently has been almost as confusing and frightening as it was those many years ago. Although I have read the Book of Mormon several times over the twenty years I've been a member, at this time I needed to hear the words of those dear friends from the dust whisper the peace and strength of the gospel to me again.

This reading has strengthened my testimony that Mormon truly saw our day, and that he, through divine inspiration, gleaned out the precious words we needed. It has also helped me to see more than ever that you are to hate the sin, but love the sinner. And that it is love for our brothers and sisters that will win them back, as the great missionaries of the Book of Mormon proved over and over. Love and service—the true examples that Jesus Christ left us—are the first stepping-stones on the path to exaltation.

This was the most wonderful assignment I've ever been asked to fulfill. Thank you again for the challenge.

"Something I Could Rely on Unconditionally"

I accepted your invitation to read the Book of Mormon this year prior to stake conference. I'm very glad I did.

Though I have read it cover to cover many times before, in some way or another every time is like the first time. This time I think what struck me the most was the thoroughness of the book. By the time you reach the end you realize that every important lesson you need to spiritually thrive in today's world, and to find joy and eternal life, has been taught to you in great clarity many times over. It is such an astounding book, and I marvel at it more now than I ever have.

I also, as you suggested, put Moroni's promise (Moro. 10:3–5) to the test once again. I felt a little sheepish in doing so—I was asking the Lord for something I already had. But still the peaceful, uplifting, reassuring feeling came to me that this book was something I could rely on unconditionally—an iron rod to guide my family and me through the mists of darkness in today's world. How grateful I am for it, and for my testimony of it!

During this same time, my wife and I also read our children's illustrated Book of Mormon series with the kids. Every night they look forward to reading their scriptures before going to bed, and the lessons and characters of the Book of Mormon have become a part of their walk and talk much more than I thought they would at this age.

Back when I was investigating the Church, I was shocked at the audacity of Joseph Smith's statement that "the Book of Mormon was the most correct of any book on earth." But now, and particularly after this most recent reading, that fact is crystal clear to me. I guess what I am shocked at now is that anyone could read the book through with "real intent" and *not* come to know of its truth.

CHAPTER 2

THE MAJESTY OF THE LORD'S WORD

The scriptures are marvelous books, books of power. And the Book of Mormon particularly is a wonder. I discover more and more as time goes by the truthfulness of what the Prophet Joseph Smith said: "I told the brethren that the Book of Mormon was the most correct of any book on earth, and the keystone of our religion, and that a man would get nearer to God by abiding by its precepts than by any other book." (*Teachings of the Prophet Joseph Smith* [Salt Lake City: Deseret Book Co., 1938], 194.)

What a tremendous promise! This is a book we should become well acquainted with, so that we can "get nearer to God."

THE BOOK OF MORMON'S DIVINE LANGUAGE

I would like to share with you some of the things about the Book of Mormon that are unique. As I do so, please understand that we could do a similar study, with different emphases, for every book of scripture. I realize that the treatment that follows only brushes over the surface of these concepts. My purpose is not to give you a full discussion of these ideas but only to introduce them to you.

The Lord speaks in such a way as to have the greatest possible impact on the hearts of men. One of the things he does in the Bible and the Book of Mormon is to speak in a poetic form called *chiasmus*. In a chiasm the ideas of a verse or passage are expressed, then repeated in reverse order to increase emphasis and to enhance our learning.

The best way to explain chiasmus is to show a chiasm in the scriptures. Here is a passage from 1 Nephi 15:9–11, arranged in chiastic form:

A the Lord maketh no such thing known unto us . . .

  B How is it that ye do not keep the commandments of the Lord?

   C How is it that ye will perish, because of the hardness of your hearts?

    D *Do ye not remember the things which the Lord hath said?*

   C If ye will not harden your hearts, and ask me in faith, believing . . .

  B with diligence in keeping my commandments,

A surely these things shall be made known unto you.

In typical chiastic form, the passage goes in a logical sequence of ideas from A to B to C to D, then back again in reverse order. The center point of the chiasm is always the point of emphasis; in this case Nephi emphasizes, "Do ye not remember the things which the Lord hath said?"

CHIASMUS IN THE BOOK OF MORMON—NO COINCIDENCE

The amazing thing about chiasmus in the Book of Mormon is that, except for a few specialized scholars, no one in the English-speaking world knew this form of Hebrew poetry even existed until the mid-1800s. It is found throughout the Old Testament—and to a degree in the New Testament (which was mostly written in Greek, not Hebrew)—but the first widespread recognition of it came with a book published in 1854. Latter-day Saint scholars agree that there was no way Joseph Smith could have known about chiasmus.

It is no coincidence that chiasmus is found in the Book of Mormon, though, because the Book of Mormon was not written by a New York farm boy. It was written by Hebrew prophets who lived in the Americas, and later it was translated into English by the gift and power of God—with the beautiful mirroring repetition called chiasmus intact.

I have in my possession a book that identifies as many of the chiasms as have been found in the Book of Mormon. There are hundreds upon hundreds of them. Some are very simple and some extremely complex.

An example of a simple chiasm is found in the Bible: "[The] first shall be last; and the last shall be first." (Matt. 19:30.) A more complex one can be found in King Benjamin's discourse in the book of Mosiah. Latter-day Saint scholars have shown the entire speech to be a chiasm, where the second half mirrors the first half, but in reverse order.

First Nephi also seems to have a like pattern—all twenty-two chapters of it. One scholar has identified more than a hundred matching phrases or ideas on both sides of the center point, each side mirroring the other. As always, the center point gives the most important idea for the whole chiasm. What is that central phrase in 1 Nephi? ". . . The Lamb of God." What a witness to the majesty of the way the Lord has constructed his words!

We ought not let these things become the focus of our study. In fact, I would not be concerned if you never even knew they existed. But if we will read the scriptures prayerfully, these things can have an impact even if we don't know about them. It is enlightening to me to see that such things as chiasmus exist; and when I see how the Lord has constructed his scriptures, I want to treat every word and every phrase with a deeper awe and respect than I ever have before.

OTHER EVIDENCES IN THE TEXT

Once we get a deep and true glimpse at what's really in the scriptures, we will know that their words do not include any phrases or sentences that are there by chance or by accident. The Lord, being the perfect being he is, has constructed his written word in such a way that it will have a profound impact on us.

Helaman 3:14 gives us an example of this. Please note the repetition of the word *and:*

> But behold, a hundredth part of the proceedings of this people, yea, the account of the Lamanites *and* of the Nephites, *and* their wars, *and* contentions, *and* dissensions, *and* their preaching, *and* their prophecies, *and* their shipping *and* their building of ships, *and* their building of temples, *and* of synagogues *and* their sanctuaries, *and* their righteousness, *and* their wickedness, *and* their murders, *and* their robbings, *and* their plundering, *and* all manner of abominations *and* whoredoms, cannot be contained in this work.

That is a fascinating passage to me—one long sentence with eighteen *and*s in it. If someone were to write that passage in English, they would leave out a lot of the *and*s and simply use commas: "their building of ships, temples, synagogues, and sanctuaries."

So why does the Book of Mormon use all those *and*s? Because when a person writes in Hebrew, he uses conjunctions to connect the many elements of a sentence like that, and because the Book of Mormon came from a people with Hebrew roots.

Another example of Hebrew influence in the Book of Mormon is found in the use of such expressions as "river of water." In English we would simply say "a river," rather than "a river of water." To us, by definition a river has water.

Would you say "I dreamed a dream"? More likely, you'd say "I had a dream," or "I dreamed."

How about "he was cursed with a curse"? No, you'd probably just say "he was cursed."

How often can we find the expression "the iron rod" in the scriptures? Answer: Not one single time. The expression is always "the rod of iron."

How many times can you find the expression "the brass plates"? Not one. It always says, "the plates of brass."

How about "Laban's sword"? Never. It always says, "the sword of Laban."

Why does the Book of Mormon use these kinds of expressions? Because that is the way you would write these things in Hebrew, and the Book of Mormon was written by a people with Hebrew origins.

Joseph Smith said one time, "I never told you I was perfect, but there is no error in the revelations which I have taught." (*Teachings of the Prophet Joseph Smith,* 368.) I bear witness that you can have complete trust and confidence in what you find in the holy scriptures. On occasion you may find something that doesn't seem to fit. "This doesn't look right," you may say. "It doesn't match with this or that." If you find something like that, hold your judgment and wait for more light, because I am confident the error is not in the text but in our lack of vision concerning what we read.

The scriptures truly are divine; they were written by men of God who were inspired both in content and form. I love the majesty and wondrous depth of God's word. I am so grateful that our Heavenly Father, in his love, has given us these books to bless us and guide us on our way back to him.

CHAPTER 3

A PERSONAL LIAHONA

Why did the Lord give us the scriptures? Why is it important that we read them? Why do we love them? Why should we care? What is the value of the scriptures to us?

I once asked these questions in a fireside and received the following excellent responses:

• They bear witness of God the Father and his Son, Jesus Christ.

• They establish a pattern of living. If you truly desire to learn that pattern, you will find it in the scriptures—and it will help you return to your eternal home. Someone once said that the scriptures are like letters from home. They're letters the Lord has written to us with instructions on how to get back to him.

• They give daily direction as you seek for it.

• They bring solace in times of hardship and pain. They seem to have an ability to heal the soul, to bring comfort, to bring peace, to bring joy. Sometimes when you feel like your heart is about to burst, you can pick up the scriptures and read those passages that most speak to your soul; and as you do, you will begin to feel the Spirit of the Lord working within you, bringing a deep and wonderful peace.

• They help reveal the Lord's purposes.

• They show the history of people and how they acted, and

they warn us not to follow the same course. The Book of Mormon, for example, is the record of a fallen people, given so that we can clearly see what happens through the years to those who keep the commandments of God and what happens to those who do not. It's a picture painted very plainly so we won't misunderstand.

• They answer important questions. In fact, 2 Nephi 32:3 says that the words of Christ will give us answers to all questions, to everything. I believe that means the scriptures contain true principles that give us the answer to any question we could ask of the Lord—even if the answer is to "listen to the prophet" or to "seek personal revelation," which are two other sources of the words of Christ. (At times I've had a fun time with missionaries and others to see if they could ask a meaningful question the scriptures couldn't answer. They have always failed—the scriptures contain principles that govern everything you can think of. Of course, it may require deep thought, prayer, and inspiration to discover those principles and their application.)

• They offer an invitation to all to come unto Christ. In fact, that is the most basic purpose of the scriptures—to stand as a witness of Christ and to teach us how to come unto him.

• They are the very voice of God to man. Many of the passages, particularly in the writings of the Old Testament prophets and in the Doctrine and Covenants, are the actual words of Jesus Christ, in print. (That's a wonderful thing to me. The greatest part of the Doctrine and Covenants is a quote from Jesus Christ himself. Consider what a unique book it is!)

WHY WE HAVE THE BOOK OF MORMON

As we talk about the purpose and importance of the scriptures, it is appropriate to specifically focus on the Book of Mormon, which was preserved by the Lord for us in this day. President Gordon B. Hinckley once said of the Book of

Mormon: "Its narrative is a chronicle of nations long since gone. But in its descriptions of the problems of today's society, it is as current as the morning newspaper and much more definitive, inspired, and inspiring concerning the solutions to those problems." (*Ensign*, June 1988, 4.)

The Book of Mormon has had few champions like President Ezra Taft Benson. Let me share with you something of his testimony of the Book of Mormon:

> It is not just that the Book of Mormon teaches us truth; though, indeed, it does that. It's not just that the Book of Mormon bears testimony of Christ; though, indeed, it does that too. But there is something more. There is a power in the book which will begin to flow into your lives the moment you begin a serious study of the book. You will find greater power to seriously study the book. You'll find great power to resist temptation. You'll find the power to avoid deception. . . . These books contain the voice of the Lord to us in these latter days. (*Ensign*, Nov. 1986, 7, 80.)

To those words I would add the witness of Elder Bruce R. McConkie:

> Few men on earth, either in or out of the Church, have caught the vision of what the Book of Mormon is all about. Few are they among men who know what part it has played and will yet play in preparing the way of the coming of him of whom it is a new witness. . . . The Book of Mormon shall so affect men, that the whole earth and all its peoples will have been influenced and governed by it.
> . . . There is no greater issue ever to confront mankind in modern times than this: Is the Book of Mormon the mind and will and the voice of God to all men? . . .
> The voice we hear is one that whispers from the dust. It is the voice of all the . . . Nephite and Jaredite prophets. It is the voice of the Lord Jesus Christ, who ministered

among the Nephites. . . . It is the voice of doctrine and testimony and miracles. It is the voice of God speaking to
men. (*The Millennial Messiah* [Salt Lake City: Deseret Book
Co., 1982], 159, 170, 179–80, 151–52.)

President Benson used to like to say, "Brothers and sisters,
the Book of Mormon is not on trial; we are!" (See *Ensign*, Nov.
1984, 8.) What a great statement! The Book of Mormon is not on
trial as to whether or not it's true. It *is* true. We are on trial to see
if we'll come to a testimony of it.

Some years ago, I searched through the Book of Mormon to
discover the answer to two questions: "First, what is the purpose of the Book of Mormon in the latter days? Second, why
did the Lord expend such a tremendous effort to preserve the
record for our time?"

Here are some of the answers I came up with:

The Role and Purpose of the Book of Mormon in the Last Days

• It is a witness for Jesus Christ. (Certainly that has to be
listed first.) (Preface to the Book of Mormon; 1 Ne. 15:14; 2 Ne.
25:17–18.)

• It contains the fulness of the gospel. (D&C 20:9; JS-H 1:34.)

• It is the instrument of conversion. As President Benson
wrote: "Combined with the Spirit of the Lord, the Book of
Mormon is the greatest single tool which God has given us to
convert the world. If we are to have the harvest of souls, we
must use the instrument which God has designed for that
task—the Book of Mormon." (*Ensign*, Nov. 1984, 7. See also Hel.
15:7–8; D&C 3:18–20.)

• It is a standard of the Lord's values for the people. As we
search through its passages, it becomes clear that it contains the
very values of the Lord, the values we must assume and absorb,
as it were, into our own bosoms. (2 Ne. 29:2.)

• It is given to gather all nations. (2 Ne. 3:23–24.) It is an ensign to the people. (2 Ne. 30:7; D&C 39:11.)

• It is a companion witness to the Bible. In fact, the Book of Mormon testifies that if you believe the Bible, really believe it, you will believe the Book of Mormon. And if you believe the Book of Mormon, it will prove the Bible also to be true. (1 Ne. 13:24–26, 29, 40–41; Morm. 7:8–9.)

• It is given to bring people to a knowledge of their fore-fathers. (1 Ne. 15:14; 2 Ne. 30:5.)

• It is given to make known the covenants of the Father. (1 Ne. 13:23; 1 Ne. 22:7–9; 2 Ne. 3:21.)

• It is a means to assist in the salvation of the elect. (Hel. 3:29.)

• It is given to help prepare a tabernacle and a "holy city," and to prepare a people for both. (Moses 7:62.)

• It is designed to help prepare the world for the Second Coming. (Moses 7:62–64.)

• It helps us have power to discern right and wrong. (Moro. 7:16–19.)

• It will help the Church come out from under condemna-tion. (D&C 84:54–57.)

• It provides us with the new covenant. (D&C 84:57.)

• It contains the record of a fallen people, given to help us avoid their fatal mistakes. (D&C 20:9.)

• It contains the plan of opposition. (2 Ne. 2:11.)

• It shows us the enemies of Christ. (Alma 30:12–18.)

I am sure there are many more reasons than these, but this list gives us at least part of the Lord's purpose in preserving the Book of Mormon in this last day.

When I let these ideas pass through my heart and mind, I see the majesty and power with which the Lord is operating around the earth. I see how he is using this book to gather Israel and all the nations on the face of the earth. At the time of this writing, we have units of the Church or members of the Church in 159 nations. And this book, the Book of Mormon, is the instrument that is gathering them to God. We must learn how to utilize it so it will help change our very lives and the lives of those around us, drawing us all closer to God.

WHY WE HAVE THE OTHER STANDARD WORKS

At least to a degree, each of the scriptures has a different purpose. They all bear witness of Christ, of course, but they each have a different focus.

As mentioned above, the Book of Mormon is the instrument of conversion. It will lead us to Jesus Christ. It will convert us to the Lord better than any other book that exists on earth.

The Doctrine and Covenants has a different purpose. It is provided to convert men to the Lord's church. President Ezra Taft Benson said:

> The Doctrine and Covenants is the binding link between the Book of Mormon and the continuing work of the Restoration through the Prophet Joseph Smith and his successors. . . . "Search these commandments," said the Lord of the Doctrine and Covenants, "for they are true and faithful, and the prophecies and promises which are in them shall all be fulfilled. . . ." (D&C 1:37.) The Book of Mormon brings men to Christ. The Doctrine and Covenants brings men to Christ's kingdom, even The Church of Jesus Christ of Latter-day Saints. . . .
>
> The Book of Mormon is the "keystone" of our religion, and the Doctrine and Covenants is the capstone, with continuing latter-day revelation. The Lord has placed His stamp of approval on both. (*Ensign*, May 1987, 83.)

I have always loved the words the Lord uses to describe the Holy Bible. He calls it "the book of the Lamb of God." (1 Ne.

13:28, 38.) What a beautiful title! In its original form, "it contained the fulness of the gospel of the Lord." (1 Ne. 13:24.)

The Old Testament has a focus and purpose that is different from the New Testament. The Old Testament "contains the covenants of the Lord, which he hath made unto the house of Israel." It also preserves for us "many of the prophecies of the holy prophets." (1 Ne. 13:23.) The New Testament is the Apostles' record of the life and ministry of Jesus Christ, which record they bore "according to the truth which is in the Lamb of God." (1 Ne. 13:24.)

Brigham Young said regarding the Bible:

> The doctrines contained in the Bible will lift to a superior condition all who observe them; they will impart to them knowledge, wisdom, charity, fill them with compassion and cause them to feel after the wants of those who are in distress, or in painful or degraded circumstances. They who observe the precepts contained in the Scriptures will be just and true and virtuous and peaceable at home and abroad. Follow out the doctrines of the Bible, and men will make splendid husbands, women excellent wives, and children will be obedient; they will make families happy and the nations wealthy and happy and lifted up above the things of this life. (*Discourses of Brigham Young,* sel. John A. Widtsoe [Salt Lake City: Deseret Book Co., 1941], 125.)

The Pearl of Great Price truly is that—a pearl, a real pearl of great price. When this book of scripture was first announced in 1851, it was recommended for "all who appreciate the revelations of truth as hidden treasures of Everlasting Life." (*Millennial Star* 13 [15 July 1851]: 217.) Those who search its pages will indeed find hidden pearls of truth.

We emphasize the Book of Mormon as much as we do, not because it is more important than any other scripture, but because it has a different focus, which is to help us become more fully converted to the Lord. But we need all the scriptures together to give us the spiritual sustenance and blessing we need in our lives.

I am grateful for the testimony of President Gordon B. Hinckley, wherein he set forth the purposes of each of the standard works:

> The standard works are all indispensable to our understanding the things of God. The Bible provides the foundation of our faith: The Old Testament gives the word of Jehovah through his ancient prophets; the New Testament sets forth, in language beautiful and moving, the matchless life and sacrifice of the Savior of mankind.
>
> The Book of Mormon stands as an added testament of Jesus Christ. Through its pages march the testimonies of prophets of the New World. Majestic in its sweep of history, its chapters are filled with the tragedy of war, with divine warnings, and with God-given promises. It speaks as a voice from the dust to a world that needs to listen.
>
> The Pearl of Great Price supplies fascinating details missing from the book of Genesis . . . and from Matthew 24. . . . It also contains the remarkable and moving account of early events in the life of the Prophet Joseph Smith.
>
> But the Doctrine and Covenants is unique among our books of scripture. It is the constitution of the Church. . . . It is my testimony, written with solemnity and great appreciation, that this remarkable book . . . sets forth "the order and will of God" to this generation. (*Ensign*, Jan. 1989, 2, 5.)

WHAT THE SCRIPTURES ARE NOT

As we begin to turn with more commitment to the scriptures, making them increasingly a part of our lives, it is important for us to understand what the scriptures are. At the same time, we need to know what they are not.

The scriptures are not just a book or set of books. They are not just facts or history, even though they have some of that in them. They are not just a reference volume for mingling some scriptural passages into our talks or lessons. (Some of us are pretty good at that—but the scriptures are so much more.)

The scriptures are not to be used only in crises, or for Sunday Church work, or for a quick fix. Even though they can help, that's not really what they're for.

The scriptures are not boring or uninteresting. They are not for just a select few or for those with leadership callings or for those who have been called to teach Gospel Doctrine classes. They are not only for scholars but also for the common man. They will communicate to and bless children, youth, and adults. They can reach both the uneducated and the scholars.

They are not to be read simply in response to feelings of guilt or just because you know you ought to. They are to be read because you love the Lord, because you love his words of truth and counsel, and because you love to grow closer to him.

WHAT THE SCRIPTURES ARE—A LIAHONA

We have listed a number of things that the scriptures are *not*. If we were to try to define what they *are*, we could do so in just one word: *Liahona*. By that I mean that they are an instrument by which you can receive revelation. If you knew how to work the instrument, and if you had properly prepared your heart, you could take it into your hands, open it just about anywhere, and receive customized guidance from the Lord.

How can you receive *customized* guidance from the scriptures? Like the Liahona, the scriptures aren't just a self-contained physical object. When we use them prayerfully and with the Spirit, they can open doors to immense spiritual realms.

Here is what Alma said as he compared the words of Christ to the Liahona:

And now, my son, I have somewhat to say concerning the thing which our fathers call a ball, or director—or our fathers called it *Liahona*, which is, being interpreted, a compass; and *the Lord prepared it.*

And behold, there cannot any man work after the manner of so curious a workmanship. And behold, it was *prepared to show unto our fathers the course* which they should travel in the wilderness.

And *it did work for them according to their faith in God;* therefore, if they had faith to believe that God could cause that those spindles should point the way they should go, behold, it was done; therefore they had this miracle, and also many other miracles wrought by the power of God, day by day.

Nevertheless, because *those miracles were worked by small means* it did show unto them marvelous works. They were slothful, and forgot to exercise their *faith and diligence* and then those marvelous works ceased, and *they did not progress* in their journey;

Therefore, they tarried in the wilderness, or did not travel a direct course, and were *afflicted* with hunger and thirst, because of their transgressions.

And now, my son, I would that ye should understand that these things are not without a shadow; for as our fathers were slothful to give heed to this compass (now these things were temporal) they did not prosper; *even so it is with things which are spiritual.*

For behold, it is as *easy to give heed to the word of Christ,* which *will point to you a straight course* to eternal bliss, as it was for our fathers to give heed to this compass, which would point unto them a straight course to the promised land.

And now I say, is there not a type in this thing? For just as surely as this director did bring our fathers, by following its course, to the promised land, shall the *words of Christ, if we follow their course, carry us* beyond this vale of sorrow into a far better *land of promise.*

O my son, do not let us be slothful because of the easiness of the way; for so was it with our fathers; for so was it prepared for them, that if they would look they might live; even so it is with us. *The way is prepared, and if we will look we may live forever.* (Alma 37:38–46; emphasis added.)

It seems clear from this passage that the words of Christ and the Liahona are comparable to each other—each guide us and teach us truth from God. Remember that the words of Christ are those words, feelings, and understandings given us by the Holy Ghost. They consist of personal revelation, inspired counsel from living prophets, and the scriptures.

Since we're trying to learn how to make the scriptures a more influential part of our lives, let's make a comparison between the Liahona and the scriptures. Each teaches us about the other.

The Liahona	**The Scriptures**
Prepared to show a straight course to the promised land.	Prepared to show a straight course to the promised land of our Father's kingdom.
Worked according to the people's faith in God.	Work for us only insofar as we have faith in God, casting out our unbelief.
Worked by small means.	Work by small means.
Would not work when the people were slothful and forgetful to use it, failing to exercise their faith and to work with diligence.	Will not work unless we exercise our faith and do so diligently.

Marvelous works and progress ceased when the people did not express their faith or diligence. Then they were unable to travel a direct course.	Individuals and families are often unable to follow a direct course when scriptures are ignored. Trouble both temporally and spiritually, because true principles have not been learned and assimilated.
People of Lehi were afflicted with hunger and thirst because of their transgressions.	People are afflicted with various trials when they do not keep commandments they would have learned through scripture study.
A great warning: "Be not slothful because of the easiness of the way." (Alma 37:46.)	A great warning: "Be not slothful" just because it is so easy to own and read scriptures.
A caution: ". . . see that ye take care of these sacred things, yea, see that ye look to God and live." (Alma 37:47.)	Look to the words the Lord has given us in the scriptures, and then we will live.

"Do Not Let Us Be Slothful"

After speaking of the Liahona, Alma gave a vital warning to us: "Do not let us be slothful because of the easiness of the way." Of course, this warning applies to our use of scriptures fully as much as to Lehi's use of the Liahona. It's very easy to have a book in your house. It's easy to pick it up and read the words of God. In fact, it's so easy that I believe we look beyond the mark and do not realize the power that rests in the pages of our precious books of scriptures.

Some years ago I was preparing some speeches on studying the scriptures, which were to be recorded and distributed. As I struggled with the format I might use, I considered giving one talk directed to beginning scripture readers and a second talk directed to the more "advanced." But as I pondered that possibility, the Spirit almost seemed to chasten me for even having thought of such a thing. It was as though the Lord was saying to me, "The scriptures were given to all men, all women, and all children. And they don't need someone to try to divide

---

"A Guide to Living"

The Testimony of a Brother

"I've been asked to write concerning the force the Book of Mormon has on our lives.

"I don't keep track of when I begin or finish reading the Book of Mormon because I have been reading in it every day for a number of years. This book, along with the Pearl of Great Price and the Doctrine and Covenants, reveals to me the will of the Lord in plainness, clarity, and simplicity. My agency then allows me to choose to follow my Lord and Savior, Jesus Christ.

"As I read in the Book of Mormon, I find myself cast in the history I'm reading. I find that most of the text portrays circumstances relative to life today. It is a guide to living within the parameters of the commandments and principles of the gospel. I have every desire to live those principles. I'm eternally grateful to the missionary program of the Church, which brought the missionaries and the Holy Ghost into my home to reveal the truth of the gospel message."

them up into the simpler parts and the advanced parts. They're all simple."

And I knew it was true.

Now, *simple* doesn't mean they're always easy to understand or that you never have to give them any effort. Nor does it mean that there are not levels of understanding, because there are. But, at their core, the scriptures are simple, and they can be understood by anyone.

I believe that the way back to our Father is so easy that even a child can follow it. That's the beauty of the scriptures. And when people say, "I just can't understand," I think they don't really know what they're saying because even children can understand. (We'll illustrate that in the third section of this book, when we talk about family scripture reading.)

CHAPTER 4

AN UNTAPPED POWER

At one point in my Church service, before I was a General Authority, I was called to be a mission representative. This assignment required me to travel from time to time. One day I was on an airplane from the Midwest, heading home to Salt Lake City. As I often do when I board an airplane, I offered a silent prayer that the Lord would have someone sit next to me who really needed the gospel, someone I might be able to exercise a righteous influence over in the hour or two we were together. As some of the passengers came down the aisle, I saw a very handsome-looking man. I thought, "That must be the one." He passed me by. I saw a lady who looked like a very good woman, probably a mother—and she also passed me by. I kept waiting and waiting. Finally the last of the passengers boarded. One of them was a young lady in her late twenties. She was probably the most immodestly dressed, most worldly looking girl I have ever been around. You can imagine my shock when I saw that she was the one who was going to sit beside me.

I was seated on the aisle, and she sat over against the window. I thought to myself, "Well, at least it looks like she does indeed need the gospel." But, because of her immodest dress, I was a little uneasy about starting up a conversation with her.

Nevertheless, we started talking. It didn't take long for me

33

to tell her I was a member of The Church of Jesus Christ of Latter-day Saints, at which point she jumped into a tirade that lasted eight or nine minutes, nonstop, telling me of the wonderful benefits of living with a man outside the covenant of marriage. She told me she had lived with a number of different men in her life. She went on and on and on about it. Her language was crude and her manner was offensive. She even asked me some very inappropriate questions about my personal life, which I didn't feel I needed to answer.

What made it even worse is that she was saying all this loud enough for some of the people in the surrounding seats to hear it as well.

"WHAT DO YOU THINK ABOUT THAT, MR. COOK?"

After she had talked this way for several minutes, she finally said, "Well, what do you think about all that, Mr. Cook?"

I offered a silent prayer that I'd know what I should say to her, then said, "Well, you probably wouldn't want to know what I think."

"What do you mean?"

I repeated, "I just don't think you'd want to know."

"No, you were polite and listened to me," she said. "Now I really want to know what you think about what I said. Give me your opinion."

"Well, my young friend," I said, "I'll give you better than that. I'll give you what the Lord said about it." And without any other comment I opened my Doctrine and Covenants to section 42 and read to her beginning with verse 22: "Thou shalt love thy wife with all thy heart, and shalt cleave unto her and none else.

"And he that looketh upon a woman to lust after her shall

deny the faith, and shall not have the Spirit; and if he repents not he shall be cast out.

"Thou shalt not commit adultery; and he that committeth adultery, and repenteth not, shall be cast out." (D&C 42:22–24.)

Without another word, I turned to section 63, verse 16, and read: "And verily I say unto you, as I have said before, he that looketh on a woman to lust after her, or if any shall commit adultery in their hearts, they shall not have the Spirit, but shall deny the faith and shall fear."

I bore my testimony to her, speaking as forthrightly as I knew how, that the word of the Lord meant just what it said, and that it was improper, incorrect, and a sin for her to pursue the lifestyle she was pursuing. (I'm not suggesting that this is how we should always respond in such circumstances. I believe we should seek and follow the Spirit in each instance.)

She immediately stopped the conversation, turned her head to the window, and started to cry—loudly. Again, I felt a little nervous about the people around me. They probably wondered, "What is that fellow doing to that poor girl?" She continued for perhaps half an hour, just sobbing against the window and refusing to say a word. I tried three different times to start the conversation again, calling her by name and apologizing that I'd upset her, but she would not talk to me.

Finally we arrived at her destination, and I stood up in the aisle for her to walk out. As she walked by she whispered, "You are right, Mr. Cook," and then moved on down the aisle.

I never heard from her again. I have no idea what became of her, but I do know, without a doubt, that the Lord spoke to her that day. I certainly could not have touched her that way. I believe those words of the Lord, as found in the scriptures, penetrated that young woman's heart, and she knew that what I had said was true.

I bear witness of the power of the Lord's words in the scriptures. If we will use them, they can powerfully affect the hearts of men. Just as surely, they can bring eternal blessings to us and our families.

Why Do We Struggle to Search the Scriptures?

If the scriptures are as powerful a blessing as we say they are (and they are), why is it so hard to consistently read them? Why do we struggle so much with ourselves and our families to be able to read as regularly as we ought to? What are some of the obstacles that stand in the way of our not being more consistent than we are?

In the fireside I mentioned before, I asked the participants to give the reasons why they struggled with scripture reading. Here are some of their responses:

"The Lord says no man can serve two masters. Jesus repeatedly submitted his will to the will of the Father, and that's what we need to do. I think a lot of times we're pitting our will against the Father's will. It's like we're constantly struggling between doing righteous works and unrighteous works."

"One reason is that it's hard to find time in the lifestyle we have now. We often feel too busy. Another is that sometimes it's hard to learn to understand what they're really saying and how they can speak to you. Some people try to read and understand, but they feel they just don't get it."

"I think sometimes we can't see the forest for the trees. Sometimes the little things get in the way, and you don't realize that that one big thing—studying the scriptures—would take care of the little things."

"I agree. We're out of focus. The scriptures have the answer to our problems, but we struggle around, as it were, in the branches of a tree instead of staying with the roots that would give us the answers we need."

"One obstacle that comes to my mind is television. Some of us are so wrapped up in watching television that there isn't time to read the scriptures. We're too busy using our time somewhere else."

"I think we're afraid of the scriptures. We don't understand their language. We hear some of those words and they seem strange and odd to us, and it scares us away. If we could learn the language of the Lord we'd be more comfortable with the scriptures."

"When you're younger, you just think, 'Well, I've heard that all before. I've read it. It says the same things over and over again, and I've heard it all.' I've even heard some people say, 'I've already read the Book of Mormon. I don't need to read it again.' Of course, those attitudes are wrong, but they still get in the way."

"Some people say the books are too long. Or that they forget everything they read, so why bother?"

Reasons or Excuses?

These concerns are fairly common to many of us. But in the end I am afraid they're more excuses than legitimate reasons. I don't suppose these excuses would sound very convincing to the Lord if we used them to explain why we did not give more time and effort to studying his holy words.

In addition, I believe the Lord has given us an answer to each of these objections. For instance, if we struggle to remember what we read, the Lord promises to quicken our memories. In John 14 he says,

"But the Comforter, which is the Holy Ghost, whom the Father will send in my name, he shall teach you all things, and bring all things to your remembrance, whatsoever I have said unto you." (V. 26.)

What a great promise! If we are struggling to remember the things of God, we can pray to the Lord specifically for help with our scripture reading. He will help us to learn how to better apply and internalize what we're reading—and he will help us to not forget what we're learning.

I suspect that all the excuses given before could be boiled down to just two. I found these as I searched the scriptures asking, Why is it that we have such difficulty spending more time in the scriptures?

Reason number one is *unbelief.* Deep down, many of us really don't believe that the scriptures will help us solve the problems we're facing. Or maybe we feel that they are not as literal as we thought. Or maybe we're not sure the scriptures are really from the Lord. If we had faith, we would be reading them more.

The second reason is *pride.* This attitude says, I don't want to admit to others how little I know, so I pretend I already know enough. I don't want anyone to find out how unskilled I am with the scriptures, so I say to myself (and maybe others) that I already know them enough.

Those two weaknesses, unbelief and pride, keep many of us from searching the words of the Lord. We may explain our reasons in many other ways, but I believe unbelief and pride are often at the core.

"CLOSER TO THE SPIRIT"

The Testimony of a Brother

"Reading the Book of Mormon these last 4½ months was a welcome and needed assignment for me. At the end of many stress-filled days, I was able to feel myself pull closer to the Spirit."

THE CHURCH UNDER CONDEMNATION

It is clear to me that the Lord isn't very pleased with our lack of regard for his scriptures. This is made plain in Doctrine and Covenants 84:

"And your minds in times past have been darkened . . ." Why? "Because of unbelief, and because you have treated lightly the things you have received." What have we treated lightly? What have we received? As we see in verse 57, he is talking particularly about the Book of Mormon.

The Lord then continues by saying, "Which vanity [another word for that might be *pride*] and unbelief have brought the whole church under condemnation. And this condemnation resteth upon the children of Zion, even all." How many of us are under condemnation? All of us.

The Lord wants us to know in no uncertain terms that he is not pleased. We are under condemnation, he says, because we have treated the Book of Mormon lightly.

"And they shall remain under this condemnation until they repent and remember the new covenant, even the Book of Mormon and the former commandments which I have given them, not only to say, but to do according to that which I have written." (D&C 84:54–57.)

As we read on, we learn the Lord's requirements for removing ourselves from the condemnation. His principal prerequisites are that we repent and remember the Book of Mormon (as we see above), that we remain steadfast in our minds, and that we open our mouths and freely testify of the truthfulness of the book and the principles it teaches. Here is what he says:

> For I will forgive you of your sins with this commandment—that you remain steadfast in your minds in solemnity and the spirit of prayer, in bearing testimony to all the world of those things which are communicated unto you.

Therefore, go ye into all the world; and unto whatsoever place ye cannot go ye shall send, that the testimony may go from you into all the world unto every creature. (D&C 84:61–62.)

It is important to note that this same passage is followed by a wonderful promise: if we will respond to this invitation from the Lord, he will greatly increase the gifts of the Spirit that shall be poured out upon the entire Church. (See D&C 84:65–73.) We see, then, that if we will immerse ourselves in the scriptures, we will not only remove ourselves from the condemnation but we will also begin to grow and be blessed in many ways.

PERSONAL STUDY

A KEY TO REVELATION AND PEACE

CHAPTER 5

HEARING THE LORD'S VOICE THROUGH THE SCRIPTURES

One of the great blessings of the scriptures is that they enable us to hear the voice of the Lord. As I explained earlier, they guide us just like a Liahona. In fact, in my judgment the primary reason we read the scriptures is to hear the voice of the Lord speaking to us, giving us revelation and instruction and causing us to have those deep feelings of peace and love that come through the Spirit.

But what does it mean to hear the voice of the Lord through the scriptures?

A passage in the Doctrine of Covenants gives us a key. These verses tell us that the scriptures truly are the voice of the Lord:

> These words are not of men nor of man, but of me; wherefore, you shall testify they are of me and not of man;
>
> For it is my voice which speaketh them unto you; for they are given by my Spirit unto you, and by my power you can read them one to another; and save it were by my power you could not have them;
>
> Wherefore, you can testify that you have heard my voice, and know my words. (D&C 18:34–36.)

This wonderful passage tells us that the Lord's voice not only gives the scriptures in the first place, by revelation, but also that when we read them we hear his voice anew. I bear testimony that there is not one person on earth who has read the scriptures humbly who has not heard the voice of the Lord. Let me emphasize that: Every person on earth who has read the scriptures with a humble and pure heart has heard the sweet whisperings of the Lord's voice to him.

If this is true, and I know it is, how can we receive this blessing? What do I have to do so that those spiritual impressions will come into my mind as I read, so that those feelings will come into my heart? What do I have to do so that my mind can be enlightened and my soul enlarged? How can I cause the word to become delicious to me, as Alma said in Alma 32:28?

A PATTERN FOR HEARING THE LORD'S VOICE

There is a pattern we can follow that will help us to hear the voice of the Lord as we read the scriptures. I don't presume that this pattern is the only way to do it, but I know it has worked for me, my family, and hundreds of other people who are trying to better hear the voice of the Lord or feel the words of the Lord while they're reading.

This pattern is so easy to understand even a child can follow it. It involves four very simple suggestions. I'll introduce them here, and then we'll spend more time on each one.

First, we need to prepare ourselves by praying in faith—not just once in awhile, but every time we read. I learned this principle from my older brother when I was twelve years old, when I first received the gift of testimony. "Gene," he said, "you ought to pray over every page." I took that literally. When I ran into a verse I didn't understand, I offered a prayer: "Heavenly Father, I don't understand this very well. Please help me understand." Many times my mind was enlightened immediately as a result of my prayer. Sometimes the answer didn't come until later. I learned that if I would keep reading, however, I would often find the answer.

Second, we need to prepare ourselves by humbling ourselves. A humble spirit can more readily be in tune with God's Spirit. We can humble ourselves by:

- Remembering how truly merciful the Lord is to us in our sins and weaknesses.
- Letting our hearts be filled with gratitude for all the Lord does for us.
- Realizing how dependent we are on the Lord for his gifts and his blessings.

Third, we need to search diligently as we're reading. Again, even a child can learn to search diligently if he is taught the skills:

- Ponder while you're reading.
- While you're reading, continually ask the Lord questions about the verses and give him a chance to answer.
- Seek to discover the patterns the Lord has given us in the scriptures. (Even this part is not too hard for children. I know because my own children have been able to learn them quite readily.)
- Mark and cross-reference the things that are important to you.
- Apply what you are reading to yourself.

Fourth, we need to obey the truths we are learning. If you learn gospel principles but do nothing with them and don't change, the Lord will be less likely to give you more. The converse of that statement is this: if you incorporate into your life the things you are learning, and repent and change, the Lord will immediately give you additional light and truth.

The Lord's response, in either case, is based on his great love for us. If he gave us too much new revelation and we couldn't live up to it, the revelation would be a burden and not a blessing. So, to protect us and at the same time to help us to grow, he gives us line upon line, precept upon precept, a little

bit here and a little bit there. As quickly as we have applied a
new truth in our lives, he will give us more—but not sooner, so
that it won't be to our condemnation. If you want to receive
more revelation from God and hear his voice much more frequently, the key is to obey what you have already received.

*As part of being obedient, we need to show the Lord that we
esteem his truths to be of great worth.* Here are some suggestions
that might help. (Again, I will give just a brief overview here,
with more details later.)

- We can ponder what we've read more fully, applying it to
all facets of our lives.
- We can record the truths we've learned so we won't forget them. That will show the Lord that we respect his
word and take it seriously.
- We can memorize passages that are particularly important to us. As we commit a scripture to memory, repeat-
ing it over and over again as we go about the activities of
our lives, the Lord will help us to apply it in our lives.
- We can share the truth with others. We have often been
told that until you are able to share a truth, it is not yours.
You may think you fully understand something, but if
you are unable to share it with someone else you
probably don't have the understanding you think you do.
But as you share, trying to help someone else to understand, you will find you're able to learn much more.

When you have done the things I've just described—pray,
humble yourself, search, and then obey what you learn (and I
repeat that even a child can do these things)—you can know
that, in the process, you will have heard the voice of the Lord
speaking to you. The scriptures will have an increasing influence on you day after day. And you will begin to experience the
mighty change of heart we read about in the scriptures. (See
Mosiah 5:2; Alma 5:12–13.)

Is it hard to learn to hear the voice of the Lord as we read his word? I believe it is not. It is simple, but it does take discipline for us to do it.

With that introduction, let's take a more detailed look at some suggestions (a pattern) for hearing the Lord's voice.

PREPARATION TO RECEIVE THE WORD

Before we can hear the voice of the Lord through the scriptures we have to prepare ourselves. I like the expression found in Alma 32: "they were in a preparation to hear the word." (V. 6.) We must do the same thing with our hearts—let them be "in a preparation to hear the word."

An account in 3 Nephi will help us to better understand this principle. After the great earthquake at the time of the crucifixion of Christ, " . . . there were a great multitude gathered together, . . . marveling and wondering one with another, . . . And they were also conversing about this Jesus Christ, of whom the sign had been given concerning his death."

While the people were so gathered, "they heard a voice as if it came out of heaven; and they cast their eyes round about, for they understood not the voice which they heard." The voice was neither harsh nor loud, but it was a "small voice" that "did pierce them to the very soul, and did cause their hearts to burn."

Even though this voice was very impressive to them, they did not understand the words because their hearts were not prepared. This happened a second time, and still "they understood it not."

We can have this same kind of experience when the Lord tries to speak to us through the scriptures and through his Spirit; if we haven't prepared our hearts we often will not receive the message.

But when the voice came the third time they "did open their ears to hear it," and finally they understood. It was the voice of the Eternal Father bearing record of his Son: "Behold my Beloved Son," the voice said, "in whom I am well pleased, in whom I have glorified my name—hear ye him." (3 Ne. 11:1–7.)

The people heard the voice the third time because they finally took action—though it was internal and invisible, they took action just the same: they sought to hear by opening their ears. The same is true of reading the scriptures. We have to take initiative and open our hearts or we will not hear the voice.

A number of years ago I prayerfully read that passage and asked the Lord, "What do I have to do to open my ears even more than I have?" As I prayed and searched for an answer, the Lord gave me a beautiful response through another scripture, an approach he commonly takes.

In wonderfully clear words, two verses in Doctrine and Covenants 136 describe this process of preparing your heart to hear the voice of the Lord:

"Let him that is ignorant . . ." Who is the Lord speaking to here? All of us. All of us are ignorant in comparison to the Lord.

"Let him . . . learn wisdom . . ." What does the Lord mean by wisdom? (As we'll discuss later, you've got to keep asking questions as you read.) If the world were going to tell you how to get more wisdom, they would probably say, "Get an education. Study. Learn from your experience. Read books." Interestingly, none of those is the approach the Lord recommends in this scripture. Instead, as this passage continues, it tells us how to get wisdom and how to hear the voice of the Lord:

> Let him that is ignorant learn wisdom by [1] humbling himself and [2] calling upon the Lord his God, that his eyes may be opened that he may see, and his ears opened that he may hear;
>
> For my Spirit is sent forth into the world to enlighten the humble and contrite. (D&C 136:32–33.)

What a testimony! If we want to hear the voice of the Lord, if we want to have his wisdom poured into our hearts, the Lord tells us how—we must humble ourselves, and we must call upon the Lord.

PREPARE YOURSELF THROUGH PRAYER

Once when we were having family scripture study, one of the children asked, "Why do we have to pray when we're reading the scriptures, Dad? Why can't we just read?"

We were studying the Doctrine and Covenants at that time, and that is where we found our answer: "And they shall give heed to that which is written"—meaning the scriptures—"and pretend to no other revelation; and they shall pray always that I may unfold the same to their understanding." (D&C 32:4.)

According to that verse, what will happen if you fail to pray about the scriptures? The Lord will not unfold their meaning to you. If you want to unlock the secrets of the scriptures, you have to pray about them as you read. I recommend that each day, before you open your book and start reading, you first pray for understanding.

We've tried to teach our children about these things, explaining that they ought to offer a very humble and very specific prayer to the Lord. "Father, help me to understand. Open my heart. Help me be more humble. Remove this unbelief or lack of faith that I struggle with. Please open my heart. Write upon my heart the things that thou wouldst tell me." If we will fervently pray in that manner, I bear testimony that something wonderful will happen spiritually. The Lord will begin to speak to you, just because you asked.

Some years ago, motivated by one of the Brethren, I did a study of the first thirty or forty sections of the Doctrine and Covenants, revealed when the Church was being organized. As I read, I asked one question throughout: What seemed to be the

Lord's greatest concern about the people in those early days? To me, the answer is evident because it is in almost every section. To paraphrase: "My people will not ask me. They go on acting like they know the answers. They won't ask. If they would just ask, I would tell them, but few will ask."

The way we ask is to pray. If we will humbly pray, in faith, that the Lord will unfold the scriptures to our minds, the blessing will come.

In Part 3 of this book, when we discuss reading the scriptures as a family, you will find some specific suggestions on how to help your family pray with feeling together before you read. Such prayer has as much power to bring about a spiritual family scripture reading session as anything I know.

PREPARE YOURSELF THROUGH HUMILITY

When Alma saw that the poor among the Zoramites were prepared to hear the word of the Lord, he noted that it was their humility that had prepared them. As it says in Alma 32:6: ". . . he beheld that their afflictions had truly humbled them, and that they were in a preparation to hear the word."

We find this principle presented in another way in the book of Moroni, in the promise recorded in chapter 10. Some people have always thought of this promise as applying only to those who are seeking a witness of the truthfulness of the Book of Mormon: "When I first read the Book of Mormon, here is what I had to do to get a testimony, but I already have a testimony so these verses don't apply to me any more." That is a short-sighted and limiting view.

The truth is that this promise tells all of us how to hear the voice of the Lord in scripture. We begin by humbling ourselves and praying. Here is the first part of Moroni's challenge to us:

> Behold, I would exhort you that when ye shall read
> these things, if it be wisdom in God that ye should read

them, that ye would remember how merciful the Lord
hath been unto the children of men, from the creation of
Adam even down until the time that ye shall receive these
things, and ponder it in your hearts. (Moro. 10:3.)

When Moroni says "ponder it in your hearts," what is he
referring to? What is it we are to ponder in our hearts? The
answer is the Lord's mercy—how merciful he has been to each
of us, to all mankind, from
Adam until now.

"WILLING TO PUT IN THE TIME"

The Testimony of a Sister

"I love the scriptures. I
love what my Heavenly
Father teaches me when I
am willing to put in the
time. The inspiration that
comes is so special. Any
problem I have can be
solved through the
scriptures. When I read
and study them daily, my
day goes well. When I
happen to miss a day,
nothing seems to go
right. Because I love the
scriptures, I know in a
small way how Lehi
must have felt when he
wanted his family to
partake of the fruit."

Why would Moroni
encourage us to ponder the
mercies of the Lord before
we ask for a testimony? Because if we do, with sincere
hearts, we will begin to feel
more humble. We will count
our blessings, seeing how
patient and merciful he has
been with each of us in our
sins, how quick he has been
to forgive and help us along
the way. When we have that
kind of heart and start to
pray about what we've read,
a testimony will come quickly.

In the same way, if we
will ponder the mercies of
the Lord and humble our-
selves before we study the
scriptures, it will help us prepare our hearts to hear the
voice of the Lord.

This is not something we
should do only from time to

time. As I noted, most of us think of Moroni's challenge as a one-time thing—but what if we were to ponder the Lord's mercies *every time* we read? "Behold, I would exhort you that *when* [meaning, perhaps, *each time*] ye shall read these things, . . . that ye would remember how merciful the Lord hath been . . . and ponder it in your hearts." (Moro. 10:3; emphasis added.)

If we were to do that, our hearts would be filled with gratitude, we would be humbled, and we would be in a position to receive even greater blessings from the Lord.

In the next verse Moroni tells us to pray. He begins by saying, "And when ye shall receive these things." Please note that here he changes the verb from *read* to *receive*. As I've sought to understand that verb, I feel that *receive* means to take something into my heart and not just my hand or my head, to say humbly, "I accept this word." It means to humble myself before the Lord and to receive his word inside myself.

> And when ye shall receive these things, I would exhort
> you that ye would ask God, the Eternal Father, in the name
> of Christ, if these things are not true; and [now he gives
> some conditions to our asking] if ye shall ask [1] with a sin-
> cere heart, [2] with real intent, [3] having faith in Christ, he
> will manifest the truth of it unto you. (Moro. 10:4.)

This is not just the pattern for receiving a testimony of the Book of Mormon, though it is that. It is also the pattern for hearing the voice of the Lord each time you read. If you will humble yourself and truly pray, doing it with real intent, with faith in Christ, doubting nothing, he will speak to you and manifest by the power of the Holy Ghost that which you want to know. In other words, your Liahona will begin to work for you because, as it said in Alma 37, you have used it with much faith and exercised extreme diligence.

These, then, are the principles of preparation. Now we will move on to the actual process of hearing the Lord's voice as we read.

SEARCH DILIGENTLY: PONDER AND QUESTION

The Lord will bless us with understandings, with answers, with impressions—with his voice—as we search his word with diligence. Perhaps the first thing we need to do as we search is to have our minds fully engaged in the reading process. As we study, we ought to be thinking deeply about what we are reading—we ought to be pondering. At the same time, we would do well to let our reading be punctuated with many questions, as we probe the true meaning of his words.

PONDERING AS YOU READ

Perhaps a good way to explain the principle of *pondering* is to use an example. One I like is Ether 12:27:

> And if men come unto me I will show unto them their weakness. I give unto men weakness that they may be humble; and my grace is sufficient for all men that humble themselves before me; for if they humble themselves before me, and have faith in me, then will I make weak things become strong unto them.

How do you ponder that verse?

You could look up some of the cross-references. Maybe you are not clear on what Moroni means by the words *weakness* or *humble* or *grace* or *sufficient.* By searching cross-references, you can get a better understanding of what the verse means.

You could go to the Topical Guide. I have had people say to me, "Elder Cook, I don't even know where to look to find additional information on a verse. I don't know even one other scripture." And I answer, "Well, that's why you have that tremendous index in the back of your Triple Combination, and that's why you have the Topical Guide." If we were to look in those sources under *Grace* or *Humility* or *Weakness,* we'd find many scriptures that would help us to get a better grasp on what the Lord is telling us in Ether 12:27.

Another approach is to pull the verse apart into small phrases, which you can then examine in your mind. "If men come unto me . . ." How does one come unto Christ? Is it just a matter of getting baptized or making covenants? Or must we also come unto him with all our hearts? Where am I in terms of coming unto Christ? How can I do better? If we will ask such questions humbly and prayerfully, with an honest desire to know the answers, the Lord will help us to understand.

One could write a whole book on pondering, but it is really not necessary, because if we will try with honest hearts, the Lord will teach us how to ponder.

I do want to add one more important point, however. *Pondering is a form of prayer.* Pondering and prayer are so tightly linked that when I start to ponder I automatically offer a silent prayer: "Help me understand this, Heavenly Father. Help me to know what this means. I'm anxious to change." I have offered such a prayer many times. "I want to repent. I want to change. I want to be better. Help me understand what I should do next."

I have seen even little children do this. As you read with them in your family scripture reading time, maybe you can help them see that sometimes they are not in the Spirit or very humble and that they too can change and repent. It is a clear and simple principle. But the blessing is based on our willingness to ask.

ASKING QUESTIONS AS YOU READ

The next element of searching diligently is to ask questions as you read. We have already seen how asking questions can be a part of pondering. But it is so important that it deserves further discussion.

I have become convinced that the scriptures are mostly an answer book. Virtually every verse has one or more answers to important questions. But would you like to read a math book that has answers to multiplication problems—but no questions? Of course not. You'd be reading "forty-eight, . . . one hundred and fifty-two, . . . oh, here's a good one, thirty-six." Such a book would be neither interesting nor helpful because you wouldn't know what the original problem or question was. To get meaning you would need to combine the original question with the present answer.

One of the greatest truths I know about reading the scriptures is that you have to continually ask questions, over and over again. Why? Because that will help us to combine the Lord's answers with the right questions, to our own profit and learning.

What might be our mode of questioning? Two kinds of questions are particularly helpful: questions we ask ourselves as we read and questions we ask of the Lord.

Questions We Ask Ourselves

Let's continue with our example from Ether 12:27 to see how asking questions will help us to understand and to grow.

> And if men come unto me I will show unto them their weakness. I give unto men weakness that they may be humble; and my grace is sufficient for all men that humble themselves before me; for if they humble themselves before me, and have faith in me, then will I make weak things become strong unto them.

What would be some questions we could ask about this verse?

" . . . *if men come unto me*":

What does it mean "come unto me"? How do I do it? When do I do it? What is the role of ordinances and covenants? What is the role of the heart? Where are some passages that will show me how to do it? Have I truly come unto Christ, or is there more I need to do?

" . . . *I will show unto them*":

How will the Lord "show unto" me? When will he "show unto" me? Why would he show something to me? Has he shown me something already and I didn't pay attention?

" . . . *I give unto men weakness*":

What is weakness? How can I find out? Do I have that? Have I always had that? Do I have weakness I'm not even aware of? How do I get rid of it? Why does it say *weakness* instead of *weaknesses?* Is there a difference? Why would the Lord, who loves me, give me weakness anyway?

" . . . *that they may be humble*":

What is humility? Why does the Lord want me to be humble? How can I know when I'm humble? What do I need to do differently to have the humility the Lord desires in me?

" . . . *my grace is sufficient for all men*":

What is grace? How do I obtain more of it? What does it mean to have "sufficient" grace?

I hope you can see what a powerful tool asking questions is. Without even completing the verse, we have illustrated more than twenty good questions, questions that matter—and we could do that same thing throughout the scriptures.

Learning from the Lord

I bear testimony that if we humble ourselves in preparation to hear the word, if we read prayerfully, and then if we start searching and asking questions, the Lord will give us answers.

But we must remain open to what the Spirit wants to teach us. If we ask questions and then listen carefully to the still small voice, we might learn things about the scriptures—and about ourselves—that we never had supposed.

In this learning and growing process, we can be confident that the Lord won't give us more than we can handle. If we are humbly praying to change, he will help us understand what we need to do. And he will do it in such a gentle way that we will be able to handle it. He is perfect in his wisdom, and though he may shake us, he will never completely overwhelm us with what he tells us.

I remember at one point in my mission I decided to make a list of all my sins so I could repent of *everything* I had ever done wrong. When I got to about sixty-seven, I felt so depressed I didn't feel like going on. I realized that my approach was wrong. We can really work on only a few things at once.

We need to be careful what we focus on. If we are always focusing on weaknesses or failures we might not be able to come to our strengths and successes. The Lord doesn't want us to put ourselves down so far that we get discouraged. Instead, as we learn from this wonderful passage in Ether 12, he wants us to come unto him, to let him reveal to us the things he would have us focus on, to be humble, to have faith in him, to receive his grace, and then, through him, to become strong.

USING THE LORD'S DEFINITIONS

When we ask and answer questions, we need to be sure we are defining words the way the Lord does. For example, some people feel that the word *humble* suggests we should view ourselves as weak or unimportant (which is a false conception), while others say *humble* means being teachable (which is correct, but true humility is so much more). When the Lord talks about being humble, he is talking about how we view ourselves in relation to him. Are we self-sufficient in spiritual things, or do we rely on the Lord? True humility is having an awareness of our dependence on Christ.

As we seek out answers from the scriptures, we need to be very careful not to use our own definitions for words, following preconceived notions or perhaps what we think we learned in a Primary or Sunday School class. We can't even rely on a dictionary definition. Instead, we need to find out what the Lord means. (I'll cover the idea of definitions in more detail in the chapter on scripture patterns from the Lord.)

Asking Questions—A Personal Example

Some years ago I had an experience that truly impressed upon me the power and blessing of asking questions as we read scriptures.

I was reading Ether 12:27, which we've just discussed, and asking myself, Did the Lord actually give me my weaknesses? If he did, why would he? Doesn't he want us to grow and develop and become like him? And isn't he perfect? Why, then, would he give me weaknesses?

As I travel about the Church I have heard this scripture quoted or referred to many times, and in almost every instance the person quotes it as saying that the Lord gives us weaknesses. You've probably had the same experience.

But as I began to seek an answer to my questions, one day I noticed that I had been misreading the verse. Moroni doesn't say that the Lord gives unto me weaknesses. In fact, the word *weaknesses* doesn't appear anywhere in the scriptures at all (it does in three chapter headings, but never in the scriptures themselves).

Instead, Ether 12:27 refers to our *weakness*. So what's the difference? As I began asking questions, I came to an insight that has been a great blessing to me. I came to understand how the

Lord defines *weakness*. I believe his definition is quite different from what most of us have been taught.

I always had a hard time thinking the Lord made me impatient, for instance, which is one of my weaknesses. Why would he make me impatient—just to give me the experience of overcoming it? But certainly I'm imperfect enough without his help—why would he add to my imperfections? It just didn't make sense.

Then I discovered that I had been misreading the verse. The Lord didn't give us *weaknesses* (impatience, laziness, anger, lust, and so forth). But he did give us *weakness*. That weakness has more to do with the state of mortality than with individual character flaws. When you were a spirit you didn't have your mortal weakness. But the Lord gave us bodies in a fallen state—which is a *state of weakness*—because that is the only way we could become as he is.

Two other scriptures give us insight into this principle. The brother of Jared prayed:

> Now behold, O Lord, and do not be angry with thy servant because of his weakness before thee; for we know that thou art holy and dwellest in the heavens, and that we are unworthy before thee; because of the fall our natures have become evil continually; nevertheless, O Lord, thou hast given us a commandment that we must call upon thee, that from thee we may receive according to our desires. (Eth. 3:2.)

The brother of Jared understood that our weakness comes "because of the fall." Still, the Lord desires to bless us.

In speaking of his "infirmities," Paul noted that he had a "thorn in the flesh," which he asked the Lord three times to remove from him. (2 Cor. 12:5, 7, 8.)

> And he said unto me, My grace is sufficient for thee: for my strength is made perfect in weakness. Most gladly

therefore will I rather glory in my infirmities, that the power of Christ may rest upon me.

Therefore I take pleasure in infirmities, in reproaches, in necessities, in persecutions, in distresses for Christ's sake: for when I am weak, then am I strong. (2 Cor. 12:9–10.)

Paul understood that it was the conditions of the flesh that constitute our weakness. But he knew what Moroni knew—that the Lord has a plan for helping us, even in our weakness. That's what Moroni was talking about in Ether 12:27. In fact, Paul took a unique view of weakness, different from what we commonly hear. He said he was actually grateful for the weakness of the flesh because it provided motivation for him to draw closer to Christ, who helped him to become strong.

CHAPTER 7

SEARCH DILIGENTLY: DISCOVER PATTERNS

Seeking patterns in the scriptures helps us to search them more deeply. It gives greater understanding of how the Lord speaks, and it helps us to see more clearly how the scriptures are constructed.

Scripture patterns provide models of the different ways the Lord presents his truths. If we can grasp the model, we can find it again and again—and our understanding of the scriptures will increase.

Many times when we read scriptures, it's as if we were looking at a box with sixty-four squares. We read a verse and say, "Aha!

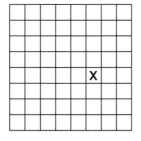

Now I understand verse 4. I finally get it." What we do not realize is that we filled in only one of the sixty-four squares.

Then what happens the next time we read that verse? "Hey, where did that concept come from? I didn't notice that before. Well, *now* I understand verse 4. I think I've got it now." But we still don't understand the whole thing. Instead, we've simply filled in another of the sixty-four squares.

Then what happens the next time we read? Again and again the Lord reveals truths until we finally say, after we have filled in all sixty-four squares, "I truly have mastered verse 4."

X	X	X	X	X	X	X	X
X	X	X	X	X	X	X	X
X	X	X	X	X	X	X	X
X	X	X	X	X	X	X	X
X	X	X	X	X	X	X	X
X	X	X	X	X	X	X	X
X	X	X	X	X	X	X	X
X	X	X	X	X	X	X	X

And then the Lord says, "Oh, do you think so?" And he brings out a three-dimensional cube that represents hundreds of additional squares on that one single verse. Then, finally, we understand that revelation is continual on that verse. It almost doesn't matter what the words are; if we continue to approach the verse humbly and prayerfully, the Lord will continue to give us additional revelations on it.

Scripture patterns will help us to break out of the two-dimensional way of looking at the scriptures and start to see them three-dimensionally. Here are twelve patterns that have helped me to better understand the meanings of the scriptures.

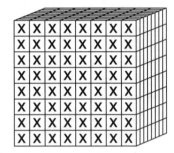

PATTERN #1: THE LORD'S DEFINITIONS

We have already taken a brief look at this idea. Now let's see if we can understand it more completely. The Lord has his own way of speaking, and he has his own way of defining certain words. If we don't learn how he communicates, we probably won't understand what he wants to say to us.

To illustrate, let's look at Doctrine and Covenants 63:53:

> These things are the things that ye must look for; and, speaking after the manner of the Lord, they are now nigh at hand, and in a time to come, even in the day of the coming of the Son of Man.

This passage includes an interesting phrase: "speaking after the manner of the Lord, they are now nigh at hand." What does *nigh* mean? Ordinarily, speaking after the manner of man, it would mean *very close*. When I was young I once read one of those passages where the Lord says, "I am at the door; the end is nigh at hand," and I thought to myself, "Wow, he must be coming this week!" But the Lord put a condition on his words by saying, " . . . speaking after the manner of the Lord." Apparently he's defining things in a different way from how man does.

Here is another example:

> Behold, now it is called today until the coming of the Son of Man. (D&C 64:23.)

What does the Lord mean by *today*, since again he is speaking after the manner of the Lord? The Lord defines today as "the period of time from right now until the point of the second coming of Christ."

One time, not long ago, I did a complete search of that word *today* in our latter-day scriptures. It's found eighteen times, and in each instance I applied the definition I just gave. In my opinion, it fits perfectly in every case. In other words, the Lord is consistent in his definition of the word.

Here is verse 24:

> For after today cometh the burning—this is speaking after the manner of the Lord—for verily I say, tomorrow all the proud and they that do wickedly shall be as stubble; and I will burn them up.

What is the Lord's definition of *tomorrow?* Essentially, it is the day of the Second Coming, when the wicked will be burned.

Another example is the word *truth.* If we are reading the scriptures and we think of truth as facts or correct information, as we were taught in school, we may miss learning some great things the Lord would teach us. Here is the Lord's definition of truth:

Truth is a knowledge of things as they are, and as they were, and as they are to come. (D&C 93:24.)

Now every time you read the word *truth* in the scriptures, remember the Lord's definition, and you'll better comprehend what he has in mind.

Another example is *chains of hell*. Is that just a poetic way of speaking, or does it really have meaning? Here is the Lord's definition, as given in Alma 12:11:

And they that will harden their hearts, to them is given the lesser portion of the word until they know nothing concerning his mysteries; and then they are taken captive by the devil, and led by his will down to destruction. Now this is what is meant by the chains of hell.

If you keep that definition in mind, whenever you see *chains of hell* you will be able to read with deeper understanding.

In one of his landmark conference talks, President Ezra Taft Benson gave us a definition of pride as it is used in the scriptures. As part of that speech, he made this very important statement: "In the scriptures there is no such thing as righteous pride—it is always considered a sin. Therefore, no matter how the world uses the term, we must understand how God uses the term so we can understand the language of holy writ and profit thereby." (*Ensign,* May 1989, 4.)

Our Father in Heaven was consistent in not using this term when he introduced Jesus Christ: "This is my beloved Son in whom I am well pleased." (See, for example, Matt. 3:17; 17:5; 3 Ne. 11:7.) He did not say "of whom I am very proud."

Some years ago I used my computer to look up *pride* in the scriptures. I found 198 instances of *pride* in the scriptures (including *proud* and *proudly*), and I patiently read them all. After hearing President Benson's testimony, I was not surprised to see that every single verse used pride in a negative or evil way.

Certainly we can use man's definitions, and we often do, but we won't if we want to speak the way the Lord does.

Of course, sometimes the Lord defines the terms he uses and sometimes he does not. What I'm recommending is that we be sensitive to the subtle ways in which the Lord helps us to know his definitions—and then to remember to use his definitions rather than our own.

Definition Indicators

I have noticed that there are three or four words that indicate a verse is going to give you a definition. One is the use of a "to be" verb (is, are, was, were, am). "Truth *is* a knowledge of things as they are, and as they were, and as they are to come." (D&C 93:24; emphasis added.)

Another "definition indicator" is the word *or*, or when the Lord says, " . . . or, in other words." For example, the Lord says, "The glory of God is intelligence, or, in other words, light and truth." (D&C 93:36.)

Another is when the Lord says "the same is . . ." For example, in 2 Samuel 5:7 it says, "Nevertheless David took the strong hold of Zion." Zion can mean many things—what is intended here? The account gives the answer by continuing: "the same is the city of David," which tells us that David took the stronghold of Jerusalem.

While we're talking about definitions, I would like to make one additional recommendation: You may also want to become familiar with the definitions of some of the archaic words used in the scriptures. For example, what does it mean to "wax"? We read in 2 Nephi, "After my father, Lehi, had spoken unto all his household, according to the feelings of his heart and the Spirit of the Lord which was in him, he *waxed* old. And it came to pass that he died, and was buried." (2 Ne. 4:12; emphasis added.) To "wax old" is to grow old.

What about a word like *twain*? The Lord said, regarding a

man and woman who had married, "And they twain shall be one flesh: so then they are no more twain, but one flesh." (Mark 10:8.) What does "twain" mean? Simply "two."

There are others. What do the scriptures mean when they say "nigh unto," or the "nethermost part of the vineyard"? What does "betimes" mean? Or "straightway"? When you come to one of those words, don't just pass it by. See if there is a helpful footnote. Or seek understanding of what the word means by looking it up in a Bible dictionary or regular dictionary. This is not as important as seeking the definitions of the Lord, but it still can be valuable.

As I have taught this in some settings, I have had people come up to me afterward and say, "Elder Cook, all this sounds a little bit complicated. I don't know if I can remember all these definitions you are giving me."

My answer: "Don't you worry about it in the least. In my judgment, the only thing you need to worry about, regardless of your age, is to humble yourself and pray as you read the scriptures. If you do that, the Lord will teach you the rest."

PATTERN #2: DOCTRINAL LISTS

A good example of doctrinal lists can be found in Alma 22:16. In the previous verse, Lamoni's father asked, essentially, "How do I obtain eternal life? How do I become born again?" Then Aaron gives this answer:

> If thou desirest this thing, if thou wilt bow down before God, yea, if thou wilt repent of all thy sins, and will bow down before God, and call on his name in faith, believing that ye shall receive, then shalt thou receive the hope which thou desirest.

This verse gives us an excellent list in answer to the question of Lamoni's father:

1. If thou desirest this thing,

2. If thou wilt bow down before God, . . . and call on his name in faith,

3. If thou wilt repent of all thy sins,

4. Believing that ye shall receive,

. . . then shalt thou receive the hope which thou desirest.

Doctrinal lists can be found throughout the scriptures. There are hundreds of them. The Lord seems to like to talk that way, and he often lists things in order. Sometimes they are in order of priority, from top to bottom, sometimes from bottom to top. When you find such a list, it will help you to understand both the passage and the doctrine better.

Another example can be found in 1 Nephi 17:3: "And thus we see that the commandments of God must be fulfilled. And if it so be that the children of men keep the commandments of God," the following will result:

1. " . . . he doth nourish them." (I've marked this in my scriptures with a "1" in the left margin.)

2. " . . . and strengthen them." (This I marked with a "2" in the margin; and so forth.)

3. " . . . and provide means whereby they can accomplish the thing which he has commanded them."

Be aware of doctrinal lists and consider marking them in your scriptures when you find them. Not only will you be thrilled to discover new truths and new relationships, but you'll also be better able to find them again at a later time.

An Insight from a List

Once our family was reading in the wars in the Book of Mormon, and one of my sons said to me, "Dad, I'm not getting very much out of this. Why are all these chapters on the wars in here anyway?"

I struggled to answer his question. Finally I said, "Well,

who knows. We may need them someday for wars that are yet to come." And I think that could very well be. There are some great strategies in there, and that could be one reason Mormon felt to include all those war chapters in the book of Alma. At the same time, I believe many verses in those pages have great spiritual lessons as well.

I gave my son the best answer I could. But then the Lord gave us all something better.

At that point in our family's experience, we had been praying very intently for a particular blessing, and we had received an answer from the Lord without realizing it. Then, that very morning, we read Alma 58:10, which not only answered my son's question but also was a powerful witness about our prayers. The words of Alma 58:10 came at a time when the Nephites were in great difficulties. They were about to lose the war, and finally they were willing to turn to the Lord.

"Therefore we did pour out our souls in prayer to God, that he would *strengthen* us and *deliver* us" (emphasis added). Again, in the left margin, I have a "1" and "2," meaning, when you're praying and asking for help, often it's for deliverance from something or for blessings of strength to bear up under a trial.

Verse 11 tells us how the Lord answered their plea: "Yea, and it came to pass that the Lord our God did visit us with *assurances* [I have a '1' in the margin there—that's one way he answers] that he would deliver us; yea, insomuch that [2] he did speak *peace* to our souls, and [3] did grant unto us great *faith*, and [4] did cause us that we should *hope* for our deliverance in him" (emphasis added).

In verse 10, then, we read what the Nephites asked the Lord for (which is what we often ask)—namely, strength and deliverance. In the next verse, we read how he helped them with assurances, peace, faith, and hope. Now, in verse 12 we discover what happens when the Lord gives us those blessings:

"And [1] we did *take courage* with our small force which we had received, and [2] were *fixed* with a *determination* to *conquer*" (emphasis added).

When the Lord breathes his peace and assurance into us, he gives us courage to act, courage that we can succeed, and a fixed determination to see it through. All this is a marvelous way of describing how his answers to prayer often work, tucked away in those war chapters. Such gems are buried all through the scriptures if we will search them out and seek understanding from the Lord.

That, then, became the answer to our family's prayers, and it became the answer to my son, who wasn't sure he was getting anything out of those chapters.

As a postscript, some years later this same boy, now in college, was having a problem, and he discovered that scripture "on his own." He didn't remember that we had all learned it together many years earlier. So he came home and gave a lesson to the whole family on it for about an hour, showing how one of his prayers was answered.

When he was finished, he said to me in private, "Dad, I'm kind of disappointed in you." He was kidding a little bit, but not too much.

I said, "Why?"

"Why didn't you ever teach me that passage?"

Then his mom and I laughed and we said, "Well, wake up, son, we did. Where were you that morning?"

That underscores another truth: many scriptures don't really come alive until you personally find them. That's why it's so important for each of us to truly seek to hear the voice of the Lord speaking to us, individually.

PATTERN #3: CAUSE AND EFFECT

A passage we used earlier can also be a good example of cause and effect. In 1 Nephi 17:3 the Lord is saying, in essence,

"If you will do your part by keeping my commandments here's what I will do."

Another example is found in Helaman 15:7. In these verses, Samuel the Lamanite is giving an answer to the question, How were the missionaries able to convert all those thousands and thousands of Lamanites?

> And behold, ye do know of yourselves, for ye have witnessed it, that as many of them as are brought to the knowledge of the truth, and to know of the wicked and abominable traditions of their fathers, and are led to believe the holy scriptures, yea, the prophecies of the holy prophets, which are written, which leadeth them to faith on the Lord, and unto repentance, which faith and repentance bringeth a change of heart unto them—
>
> Therefore, as many as have come to this, ye know of yourselves are firm and steadfast in the faith, and in the thing wherewith they have been made free. (Hel. 15:7–8.)

According to that passage, the scriptures will lead you to faith on the Lord. Reading the scriptures is the cause; faith on the Lord is the effect. Where will faith lead you? To repentance. And where will that lead you? To a change of heart. And the next step? You continue "firm and steadfast." What a beautiful example of this principle of cause and effect!

The scriptures are full of cause and effect because the Lord operates that way, which is by law. The law is in place, and if you obey it, you'll get a positive result; if you disobey, you'll get a negative result. With the Lord, both his promises and punishments are sure.

Pattern #4: If and Then

There are hundreds of examples of this pattern. Ether 12:27 has two instances alone:

If men come unto me I will show unto them their weakness . . . *if* they humble themselves before me, and have faith in me, *then* will I make weak things become strong unto them (emphasis added).

Another example is found in 2 Nephi 31:5:

And now, *if* the Lamb of God, he being holy, should have need to be baptized by water, to fulfil all righteousness, O *then*, how much more need have we, being unholy, to be baptized, yea, even by water! (emphasis added).

Here's another, found in D&C 104:56:

And *if* the properties are mine, *then* ye are stewards; otherwise ye are no stewards (emphasis added).

I did a computer search to find all the verses in the standard works that have a combination of the words *if* and *then*. I found 427! (Of course, some of these are not true if-then combinations, but most are.)

I understand that the Hebrew language will often have an assumed "if" or an assumed "then," without actually including both. English does the same. So if you see one or the other, (then) take a close look and see if the Lord is implying an actual if-then relationship, even if he doesn't come right out and say it.

PATTERN #5:
WORDS FOR EMPHASIS, ATTENTION, OR FOCUS

One of the most common Hebraisms in all the Book of Mormon is "It came to pass." That phrase occurs about thirteen hundred times in the Book of Mormon. (It occurs more than 450 times in the Bible.)

Earlier, as the book was translated into various languages, some translators took that phrase out, saying it was too repetitive. In some translations, for instance, they included the expression only the first time, then said, "Hereafter we're putting in asterisks instead of 'it came to pass,' because it's too repetitive."

Such an approach to translation is not allowed, of course, partly because "it came to pass" is an important part of the language of the Book of Mormon.

"It came to pass" is often a transitional statement. It can show the passage of time or a compression of events. In a beautiful way, I believe, it is a great testament to the modesty and humility of the Lord as well. An example will demonstrate what I mean.

If you take a young man and ask him who was responsible for his going on a mission, he might give you a variety of answers: The impressions of the Lord, the young man's parents, a priests adviser, a bishop. But is that the end of the list? Certainly not.

Who else might have influenced that young man? His grandparents, friends, a Sunday School teacher, a Scoutmaster, a girlfriend, seminary instructors, the neighbor across the street, a home teacher, a visiting teacher. We could name many, many people who have helped. What about those who have gone on through the veil? Could they also be seeking that blessing for the young man?

And how many of those people were being touched and influenced by the Lord to bless the young man in ways that would make a difference?

With all that in mind, how would we answer the question, Who is responsible for that young man going on a mission?

Perhaps the best answer, knowing that many, many people helped (especially if you were writing a record with limited space), would be to say simply: "And it came to pass that Ron went on a mission."

As I think about many of these passages in the Book of Mormon that use that simple phrase—"and it came to pass"—I stand in awe of the Lord's humility. How often he has been directly responsible for orchestrating events that have blessed people's lives—and how often he has refrained from taking credit in the scriptures!

Perhaps in the example of the missionary, the father was the one who had the greatest influence on the young man going. But a wise father would avoid drawing attention to his own efforts by saying, "And I worked hard and blessed my son over and over and finally influenced him to go on a mission." Instead, he might say, "And it came to pass that my son was influenced to go on a mission."

"And it came to pass" is a simple, powerful, modest, humble way of saying volumes. It takes the emphasis, attention, and focus from one place and puts it in another. Watch for that phrase in your reading, and you will see how effectively it serves that purpose.

Other Common Hebraisms in the Book of Mormon

The other most common Hebraisms in the Book of Mormon—as well as other scriptures—are the words *yea, behold,* and *even*. Many scriptures begin with the word, "Behold," which has the function of causing us, if we're reading thoughtfully, to slow down in our reading and pay attention. It is one of the means the Lord uses to get our attention before we race on. ("Behold" appears 3,205 times in all the scriptures.)

The word *yea* can serve the same purpose. It puts great focus and emphasis on the phrase that follows it, giving greater power to that scripture. ("Yea" is in the standard works a total of 1,526 times.)

Another is the word *even*. It is a powerful word used to capture our attention and to give focus, particularly in the Book of Mormon. Pay attention to how *even* directs your thinking as you read. You may be surprised at what you'll learn. ("Even" is found in the scriptures 2,405 times, but this number includes usages other than the one we are discussing here.)

And how much do all these things matter? The answer: They can be helpful, but ultimately they don't matter a great deal if you remember to pray and to be humble. Then the Lord will lead you as you go along. And then, even if you never knew the ideas in this chapter, it wouldn't matter. But if you do know these things, you will have a greater respect for the scriptures, and you will be able to gain greater insight as you read.

PATTERN #6: ANTECEDENTS

The word *antecedent* is a term used in grammar to indicate which noun goes with which pronoun or other substitute. By understanding the antecedents of pronouns, we can understand particular passages better.

A good example is found in 1 Nephi 3:5. The speaker in this passage is Lehi:

"And now, behold thy brothers murmur, saying *it* is a hard thing which I have required of them; but behold I have not required *it* of them, but *it* is a commandment of the Lord." (What is the antecedent of "it" in this verse? That they have to return to Jerusalem to get the brass plates.)

In an earlier chapter we talked about Moroni 10:3, which admonishes us to "ponder it in your hearts." What was the antecedent of that "it"? How merciful the Lord has been unto us. Think what we would have missed in our understanding if we had not gone back to find out what the "it" referred to.

Sometimes it is very challenging to discover the antecedent in some passages, but when you do, you will be able to decipher the scriptures much more quickly.

Here is one final example, this one more difficult. Discovering the antecedent in Doctrine and Covenants 84:19 uncovers a great truth. I commonly hear this verse quoted incorrectly because people have not sought out the antecedent. In speaking about the Melchizedek Priesthood, the Lord says, "and this greater priesthood administereth the gospel and holdeth the key of the mysteries of the kingdom, even the key of the knowledge of God." My question is, What is the key? Does the Lord tell us? He surely does as we read on:

> Therefore, in the ordinances thereof, the power of godliness is manifest.
>
> And without the ordinances thereof, and the authority of the priesthood, the power of godliness is not manifest unto men in the flesh;
>
> For without *this* no man can see the face of God, even the Father, and live.
>
> Now *this* Moses plainly taught to the children of Israel in the wilderness, and sought diligently to sanctify his people that they might behold the face of God. (D&C 84:20–23; emphasis added.)

What is the antecedent to the word *this* found in verses 22 and 23? I believe it is "the power of godliness":

"Without [the power of godliness, or personal righteousness] no man can see the face of God, even the Father, and live.

"Now this [truth about the power of godliness] Moses plainly taught to the children of Israel."

And what is the key to the mysteries of the kingdom, even the key to the knowledge of God? My understanding is that that key, again, is personal righteousness or godliness. A passage in Doctrine and Covenants 121 helps with this understanding:

> God shall give unto you knowledge by his Holy Spirit, yea, by the unspeakable gift of the Holy Ghost, that has not been revealed since the world was until now; . . .
>
> A time to come in the which nothing shall be

withheld, whether there be one God or many gods, they
shall be manifest.

All thrones and dominions, principalities and powers,
shall be revealed and set forth upon all who have endured
valiantly for the gospel of Jesus Christ. (D&C 121:26, 28–29.)

This, then, is talking about the Lord's promise that he will
give us the mysteries of godliness and the knowledge of God.
What is the key to receiving these? The Lord gives us a clue
when he says, "the rights of the priesthood are inseparably connected with the powers of heaven, and . . . the powers of heaven
cannot be controlled nor handled only upon the principles of
righteousness." (D&C 121:36.)

Personal righteousness, personal godliness helps us to
receive revelation of God's mysteries and to control or handle
the powers he gives to us.

I hope we all can see that understanding antecedents can
teach us great truths about the gospel and the meaning of the
scriptures.

PATTERN #7: REVERSE MEANINGS

With reverse meanings, we learn by seeing the opposite of
what we expected—or by seeing what's *not* in a passage, as well
as what's there.

For example, Doctrine and Covenants 107 contains a very
significant verse that had to do with the final organization of the
Quorums of Seventy of the Church. There were many reasons,
of course, why the quorums were organized—not the least of
which was a direction from the Lord that told President Spencer
W. Kimball it was time to do it. But this verse had much to do
with preparing the minds of the Brethren for that eventuality.

Here is what the Lord said in Doctrine and Covenants 107:10:

High priests after the order of the Melchizedek
Priesthood have a right to officiate in their own standing,

under the direction of the presidency, in administering spiritual things, and also [these high priests can function] in the office of an elder, priest . . . , teacher, deacon, and member.

But where's the seventy in this list? This verse does not specify that a high priest can function in the office of a seventy. Why? Because the office of a seventy is an apostolic calling. (See verses 23–26.) A seventy with the apostolic calling can function as a high priest, but not the other way around.

In this instance, we learn something valuable from what's *not* in the verse, as well as what's there.

Here are three other examples of reverse meanings.

1. How many times do you think the words *free agency* are in the scriptures? Not one single time.

Now the absence of that expression ought to shout out an important lesson to us. We must begin to have a different view of agency. The Lord never does talk about "agency" as freedom to do whatever you want. Instead, he uses the word *agency* without a qualifier, or he says it's *moral agency*. (See D&C 101:78.) We have each been taught what is right, and the Lord wants us to be agents unto ourselves according to the commandments he has given. That's very different doctrine from what we have sometimes been taught—but our understanding grows when we look at what's *not* there.

2. As important as welfare is, how many times do you suppose the word *welfare* is found in the Doctrine and Covenants? Answer: Not one single time. That again ought to shout out at us that there's something important to be learned from the absence of the word. (*Welfare* does appear in the Book of Mormon a number of times—twenty, to be exact—but in every instance it's referring to the welfare of an individual.)

3. How about the word *leadership*? It doesn't exist in the scriptures. Why? It's such an important word in our society that we'd do well to learn why it's not in the scriptures.

When we note the absence of a word or concept in the

scriptures, and then try to discover the meaning of its absence (or a reverse meaning), we can learn as much as we can about things that are there.

Brigham Young once made a helpful statement about this concept. He said the devil is capable of counterfeiting every true principle, and if you want to learn doubly, learn a principle in its true form, then see what the devil teaches by turning it around. When you know the devil's principles, you can better avoid them.

Or you can do the same thing in reverse. Notice in the scriptures what it tells us about what the devil teaches. If you can find the reverse of it, you may be able to learn a true principle.

> If true principles are revealed from heaven to men, and if there are angels, and there is a possibility of their communicating to the human family, always look for an opposite power, and evil power, to give manifestations also: look out for the counterfeit.
>
> There is evil in the world, and there is also good. Was there ever a counterfeit without a true coin? No. Is there communication from God? Yes. From holy angels? Yes; and we have been proclaiming these facts during nearly thirty years. Are there any communications from evil spirits? Yes; and the Devil is making the people believe very strongly in revelations from the spirit world. (Brigham Young, *Journal of Discourses* 7:239–40.)

I believe that's true. I believe that if we recognize Satan's counterfeits we can learn something from them. And I believe we can learn twice from the scriptures, first by looking at them frontwards, then by considering them backwards. When the Lord says, "If you keep my commandments . . ." and then makes a promise, you could very well say "and if I keep not his commandments . . ." and fill in the blank. That process teaches us far more than if we simply read what's given and don't consider any other truth.

PATTERN #8: LITERAL READING

The scriptures are literal. They really do mean what they say. In Doctrine and Covenants 36:2, for example, the Lord says to Edward Partridge, "I will lay my hand upon you by the hand of my servant Sidney Rigdon, and you shall receive my Spirit, the Holy Ghost, even the Comforter, which shall teach you the peaceable things of the kingdom."

Think of what he is saying. A bishop might place his hands upon the head of a member and say, "I now lay my hands upon you, John, as your bishop, to set you apart"—and at the same time, it would be as if Jesus Christ were saying, "It will be as if I laid my own hands upon your head. I will do it through my servant, the bishop."

Does this scripture really mean that? It really means that. If you're a priesthood holder, then, and you're giving someone a blessing, you are standing in the stead of the Lord in putting your hands on his or her head. Your hands are very literally representing the hands of the Lord.

And if you're receiving that blessing, what a great thing it is to know that the person who is officiating is standing in for the Lord.

The scriptures are literal. We must always remember that.

Another example. I love the fifth Article of Faith, which says, "We believe that a man must be called of God, by prophecy, and by the laying on of hands by those who are in authority, to preach the Gospel and administer in the ordinances thereof."

Does the Lord really mean that? Is it his will that all callings to serve God are to be given by prophecy—meaning by the spirit of revelation? Should even a Primary teacher in the nursery, for example, be called by prophecy? Or can the bishop just choose according to his own judgment—or according to desperation?

This Article of Faith, which is scripture, means what it says.

All callings *must* come by prophecy (or revelation), by those in authority. And if those in authority are acting by the spirit of revelation, which is both the pattern and the practice in the Church, then the Lord says, "Whether by mine own voice or by the voice of my servants, it is the same." (D&C 1:38.)

It is the bishop who has the keys of the priesthood in the administration of a ward. Whether he is serving with his hands or his voice, he is representing the Lord. When we as Latter-day Saints understand that, we will begin to respond very differently to our bishops than we may have before.

I bear witness again that the scriptures are literal. They have multiple meanings. They apply across time. They apply across cultures. They apply to all people, both as groups and as individuals. They can apply to Moses' day, to Christ's day, or to our own day. That is the power of the way the Lord speaks.

Literal or Figurative?

It's true that the scriptures are literal—and it's very important that we know that. Many people, for instance (even including some ministers in other churches), don't believe that Jesus was literally born of a virgin or that he was literally the Son of God. Many people don't believe that Adam and Eve were literally the first parents of our race, or that the flood in Noah's day literally covered the whole earth.

Some critics in the Church don't believe we should take literally the scripture statements that Joseph Smith translated the Book of Mormon "by the gift and power of God." (D&C 135:3.) They say instead that Joseph Smith was the author rather than the translator of the Book of Mormon, and that what he produced is a good, uplifting book but not scripture from ancient prophets.

I disagree with such views and attitudes. I believe the scriptures are literal and, if we want to know the truth, we should read them literally. When the Lord speaks about his requirements and expectations of us, I believe we should read such scriptures literally. But I do wish to add a caution to this understanding. There is also much in the scriptures that is figurative or symbolic.

For instance, when Jesus talked of our being "born again," Nicodemus asked if we need to reenter our mother's womb. Jesus explained that we must be "born of the Spirit." (John 3:3–6.) We would be mistaken if we felt that we must literally be born again in the same way we originally were born into this world. But we would also be mistaken if we ignored the Savior's explanation: We must literally be born of the Spirit, as "new creatures." (Mosiah 27:26.) We must literally be changed in our natures from fallen, carnal men and women to Saints, men and women of God. (See Mosiah 5:2; 27:24–26.)

Another example: In the book of Revelation, John talks about the second coming of Christ. He said, "His eyes were as a flame of fire, and on his head were many crowns; . . . and out of his mouth goeth a sharp sword." (Rev. 19:12, 15.) Certainly fire does not literally come out of the Lord's eyes, nor are there literally many crowns on his head, nor does a sword literally come out of his mouth. But these symbolic statements do teach us some important literal truths about Christ: He is the source of light, even controlling such great powers as the sun; he is the King of kings; and he will come forth with great judgments on the earth.

I repeat, then: Let us be cautious that we do not put literal meanings on things the Lord clearly intends to be figurative. (Though there is always an important literal meaning revealed by understanding the symbolism.) But, perhaps even more importantly, let us not put figurative or symbolic meanings on things the Lord wants us to read literally.

PATTERN #9: SUMMARY PHRASES

After the Lord has taught a concept, he sometimes stops to make a summary statement. These statements are often preceded by one or more "cue words" that help us spot them. Here are some key cue words or phrases that help me locate the Lord's summaries:

The first is *thus we see*, which is often used in the Book of Mormon. Alma 30 gives us a helpful example. After telling us about Korihor for fifty-plus verses, Mormon ends the account by saying, "And thus we see the end of him who perverteth the ways of the Lord. . . ." In one single verse he gives you a summary of fifty verses.

The phrase "and thus we see" gives us the bottom line, the moral to the story, the thing the Lord most wants us to learn and remember. When we see that phrase, we should stop and notice and ponder what we have read. ("Thus we see" occurs twenty-four times in the Book of Mormon.)

A second cue word is *thus*, standing alone. Mormon was most helpful in including many of these cues in his summaries, and I love him for it. His use of *thus* helps readers of our day to better understand the message and the meaning of the book that bears his name. (There are about 450 of these in the Book of Mormon, not counting those used in the first category.)

The last three cue words are related in their function. The first is *wherefore*, which shows cause and effect. (It occurs nearly a thousand times in the scriptures.) The second is *therefore*, which does essentially the same thing. (It occurs more than two thousand times.) And the third, which shows contrast, is *nevertheless* (344 occurrences). When I see those words, I stop and pay particular attention to the text, because often it will give a summary statement.

PATTERN #10: SIMILES

We learned about similes in English class in high school. A simile is a figure of speech in which two unlike things are compared. Usually the comparison includes the word *like* or *as*. A well-known example is found in Isaiah 35:1, "The desert shall rejoice, and blossom as the rose."

There are many wonderful similes in the scriptures—and if

we are not paying attention to the comparisons the Lord makes, we might miss some insights into doctrine and truth.

In Doctrine and Covenants 101:39, for instance, the Lord says, "When men are called unto mine everlasting gospel, and covenant with an everlasting covenant, they are accounted *as* [when I see one of these, I mark it heavily in my scriptures] the salt of the earth and the savor of men" (emphasis added). So the Lord is comparing men to salt. If you'll sit and ponder that, you'll see some deep meanings buried in there.

Another example. In Jacob 5 the Lord compares the house of Israel to an olive tree. The olive tree, therefore, represents the Lord's people, the people of his covenant. If you don't have that clear in your mind, you can read that whole chapter and say, "What is all this about anyway? I'm not getting very much out of this." But if you start out with a correct understanding of the comparison the Lord is making, you can read all the things he does with the branches of his trees (which are his people), and you will come up with a new understanding altogether of the allegory of the olive tree.

Another very powerful one is found in Abraham 3. I love this one because of a tremendous experience I once had with it. I was trying to hear the voice of the Lord as we've described here— praying, trying to humble myself, searching, and trying to obey— and I learned a great principle, all focused on one little word: *as.*

The first seventeen verses of Abraham 3 tell us about the sun, the moon, the stars, the Urim and Thummim, and how one world is above another. As I've read that passage from time to time I've thought, "Why did the Lord include these things here? Why does he want us to know these things?" I liked what I was learning, but I wasn't sure how it pertained to me. For some reason I didn't read verse 18 very carefully, and so I missed it when the Lord said, "Howbeit that he made the greater star; as [and now I know to put a big red mark on that *as*, because he is setting up a comparison], also, if there be two spirits, and one shall be more intelligent than the other, . . . There shall be another more intelligent than they; I am the Lord thy God, I am more intelligent than they all. . . . I rule . . . over all the intelligences thine eyes have seen." (Abr. 3:18, 19, 21.)

Suddenly I realized that perhaps the first seventeen verses of that chapter were not included just to give me an astronomy lesson. They were there to teach me about God—and about my relationship to him. Abraham 3 isn't really just about stars and planets—it is about the Creator and his children. Knowing that, I can now read that chapter with a completely different understanding.

There are scores of instances in the scriptures where the word *like* is used in a simile. The New Testament in particular is filled with them. It says the gospel is like a net of the sea. People are like salt that has lost its savor, or like a light on a hill. Jesus talked of the lilies and the fishes, of simple things, making comparisons. We shouldn't just read right over those, because we'll learn some powerful lessons if we'll ponder the analogies he makes, giving us tremendous understanding we otherwise would not have.

PATTERN #11: SUPERLATIVES

In a way this is another example of reverse learning, because the remarkable thing about superlatives in the scriptures is that the Lord rarely uses them. About the most he typically says about his marvelous works is that "they are of great worth." (1 Ne. 13:23.)

For example, after creating this world for his children—this wonderful, beautiful world—he said simply, with great understatement, "It was good." Then, later, he said, "It was very good." (See Gen. 1:25, 31.)

When the Lord does use superlatives, we should pay close attention: "a marvelous work and a wonder" (2 Ne. 25:17); "I will make of thee a great nation, and I will bless thee, and make thy name great" (Gen. 12:2); "For unto us a child is born, . . . and his name shall be called Wonderful" (Isa. 9:6).

The Lord's example teaches me a valuable lesson about the way I ought to speak. I ought to take care that I don't overstate things with superlatives—tremendous, stupendous, incredible. Instead of using those kinds of descriptions, the Lord generally speaks in a very modest way, declaring the truth in simple terms and letting it stand for itself.

In one of his conference talks, President Ezra Taft Benson suggested that we ought to use the language of the Lord in our teaching (see *Ensign*, May 1987, 83–84)—avoiding superlatives might be part of what we should seek to do.

PATTERN #12: ABSOLUTES

Superlatives are rare in the scriptures—but the Lord uses absolutes quite frequently. Absolutes are such terms as *always, never, all, none, every,* and so forth.

When humans use absolutes, they are most likely guilty of exaggeration, but the Lord always speaks very precisely. If he speaks in an absolute, we can be certain he means it.

Here are a few examples:

> *Always* retain in remembrance, the greatness of God, . . . calling on the name of the Lord daily, and standing steadfastly in the faith. . . . [I]f ye do this ye shall *always* rejoice, and be filled with the love of God, and *always* retain a remission of your sins. (Mosiah 4:11–12; emphasis added.)

> I am the bread of life: he that cometh to me shall *never* hunger; and he that believeth on me shall *never* thirst. (John 6:35; emphasis added.)

> Charity *never* faileth. (1 Cor. 13:8; emphasis added.)

(*text continued on page 88*)

Scripture Patterns of the Lord

Patterns help us to speak and learn after the manner of the Lord. (D&C 63:53; 64:23–24.) They are spiritual road signs and prompts to reading. Here is a summary of the patterns presented in the text, with some additional examples and scriptures.

1. **Definitions**
    A. A Few of the Lord's Definitions
       —*Nigh* (D&C 63:53)
       —*Today* (D&C 64:23)
       —*Tomorrow* (D&C 64:24)
       —*Truth, knowledge* (D&C 93:24–25)
       —*Glory* (D&C 93:36)
       —*Intelligence* (D&C 93:29)
       —*Chains of hell* (Alma 12:11; D&C 138:23)
       —*Honor/power* (D&C 29:36; 76:28; Moses 4:1)
       —*Rest* (D&C 84:24)
       —*Right way* (2 Ne. 25:28–29; Moro. 6:4)
    B. Archaic Definitions
       —*Wax:* grow, increase (D&C 45:27; 121:45)
       —*Twain:* two (D&C 45:48; 49:16)
       —*Nigh* unto: close, near to (D&C 104:3; Abr. 3:9)
       —*Nethermost* (Jacob 5:13, 14, 19, 38, 39, 52)
       —*Betimes:* early, timely, before too late (Gen. 26:31; Job 8:5; D&C 121:43)
       —*Straightway:* immediately, at once (D&C 76:47; 136:25)

2. **Doctrinal Lists—Sequential** (1 Ne. 17:3; Alma 14:1; 22:16; 58:10)

3. **Doctrinal Lists—Cause/Effect** (2 Chr. 16:12–13; Hel. 15:7–8; Moro. 8:25–26; D&C 29:40)

4. *If* and/or *Then to* **Identify Cause and Effect** (2 Ne. 31:5; Alma 37:40–41; Eth. 12:27; D&C 104:56)

5. **Words for Emphasis/ Attention/Focus**

Yea	Behold	Even
1 Ne. 18:18	1 Ne. 2:1	1 Ne. 10:4
2 Ne. 4:35	2 Ne. 1:10	Alma 32:27

And It Came to Pass	
1 Ne. 18:25	1 Ne 7:1
Enos 1:23	Jacob 5:4

6. **Antecedents** (1 Ne. 3:5; 8:20; 13:23; Moro. 10:3; D&C 84:19–23)

7. **Reverse Meanings or Absence of a Word, Phrase, Etc.**
   —*Keep my commandments/ not keep my commandments* (Alma 9:13)
   —Absence of *leadership* (0 times in the scriptures)
   —Absence of *welfare* (0 times in D&C)
   —Absence of *free agency* (0 times in the scriptures)
   —Absence of *weaknesses* (0 times in the scriptures)
   —Absence of *the Seventy* (D&C 107:10)

8. **Literal Reading** (John 3:3–6; Rev. 19:12, 15; Mosiah 5:2; 27:24–26; 3 Ne. 17:7; D&C 36:2; 135:3; A of F 5)

9. **Summary Phrases**
   —*Thus we see* (Alma 24:19; 30:60; Hel. 12:3)
   —*Therefore* (1 Ne. 1:1; 3:6; 3 Ne. 13:8, 9)

   —*Wherefore* (1 Ne. 2:16; 7:12; D&C 1:6–7)
   —*Nevertheless* (1 Ne. 13:23; 14:12; D&C 1:32)

10. **Similes**
    —*As* (Isa. 35:1; 2 Ne. 3:19; D&C 65:2; 101:39; Abr. 3:18)
    —*Like* (Matt. 13:31, 44, 47; 28:3; Jacob 5:3; Mosiah 2:38)

11. **Superlatives**
    —*Great worth* (1 Ne. 13:23)
    —*More or less* (D&C 93:24–25)
    —*A marvelous work* (2 Ne. 25:17; D&C 4:1)
    —*Good, very good* (Moses 2:25, 31)
    —*Great* (Gen. 12:2)
    —*Wonderful* (Isa. 9:61)

12. **Absolutes**
    —*Always* (Mosiah 4:11–12)
    —*Never* (John 6:35; 1 Cor. 13:8; Alma 41:10)
    —*All* (Rom. 3:23; 2 Ne. 32:3; D&C 18:11)
    —*All/None* (Mark 12:30; 2 Ne. 2:6–7; 26:33)
    —*Nothing* (2 Ne. 26:33)
    —*Every* (Moro. 7:16)
    —*No* (Alma 40:26)

(text continued from page 85)

Wickedness *never* was happiness. (Alma 41:10; emphasis added.)

Feast upon the words of Christ; for behold, the words of Christ will tell you *all* things what ye should do. (2 Ne. 32:3; emphasis added.)

Behold, the Lord your Redeemer suffered . . . the pain of *all* men, that *all* men might repent and come unto him. (D&C 18:11; emphasis added.)

And thou shalt love the Lord thy God with *all* thy heart, and with *all* thy soul, and with *all* thy mind, and with *all* thy strength: this is the first commandment. (Mark 12:30; emphasis added.)

He doeth *nothing* save it be plain unto the children of men; and he inviteth them *all* to come unto him and partake of his goodness; and he denieth *none* that come unto him, . . . and *all* are alike unto God. (2 Ne. 26:33; emphasis added.)

For behold, the Spirit of Christ is given to *every* man, that he may know good from evil. (Moro. 7:16; emphasis added.)

Why does the Lord speak in absolutes? Why does he allow no wriggle room in many of the things he says? I believe that because he is a God of law as well as a God of truth, he cannot do otherwise. Natural law is absolute—we all know how certain and infallible gravity is (things on earth *always* fall down, not up). Eternal law is just as certain and infallible, and God, in his love, tells the truth about that law.

It is the absolutes of eternal law that make it so necessary for us to have a Savior:

No unclean thing can inherit the kingdom of God. (Alma 40:26; emphasis added.)

All have sinned, and come short of the glory of God. (Rom. 3:23; emphasis added.)

Wherefore, redemption cometh in and through the Holy Messiah; for he is *full* of grace and truth.

Behold, he offereth himself a sacrifice for sin, to answer the ends of the law, unto *all* those who have a broken heart and a contrite spirit; and unto *none* else can the ends of the law be answered. (2 Ne. 2:6–7; emphasis added.)

I thank my Father in Heaven for his absolutes—and for providing a way, in our weakness, to meet his requirements. And I'm grateful for the scriptures, which clearly tell us the truth about who God is and what he requires of us.

A Caution

I have already expressed a caution about overemphasizing the things discussed in this chapter, but I would like to repeat it here. I have given these patterns because they've been helpful to me—but what if you lived and died and didn't know anything about these patterns? Would it matter? No, it would not. Because if you will be prayerful, and if you will humble yourself, as I said before, the Lord will lead you along, and he will give you what you need to know. No one should be frustrated or troubled if they can't remember all these things. On the other hand, I have learned with my own children (and I have eight of them) that even a little girl who is seven years old can understand these ideas. And if there are any she's unsure of, I suspect it's the fault of the teacher (meaning myself). I've had the same experience with all of my children.

These things can bless us if we will apply ourselves a little. But we shouldn't get frustrated or worried if they don't come easily.

CHAPTER 8

SEARCH DILIGENTLY: MARK AND CROSS-REFERENCE YOUR SCRIPTURES

I used to believe that marking and cross-referencing were nice but not essential. I feel differently now—I have come to believe that these skills really do make a difference in our ability to understand the scriptures. Even more, we should teach our children how to mark and cross-reference their scriptures. We can't just assume they will start doing it on their own. If we will school our children as we read scriptures with them, they'll develop skills that will bless them all their lives.

Why is this so important? Consider:

1. Cross-referencing increases understanding. It gives you insights you otherwise would not have had. It shows you a unity in the scriptures—and a depth.

2. Part of cross-referencing is checking the footnotes. When we find footnotes to the Topical Guide, the Bible Dictionary, or the Joseph Smith Translation, we open a door to greater knowledge and greater truth.

3. When you are marking the scriptures, trying to pick out important parts, it keeps you focused on what you're reading. It helps you answer the question, What is the most important point in this verse?

4. Marking increases understanding. When you're reading

close enough to make markings, you learn more than when you're just racing through the pages.

5. Marking helps the remembering process when you reread. If you have marked an *as* or *thus,* as we discussed in the previous chapter, you will quickly remember, on review, what it was you saw in that verse.

6. Marking helps you find things more quickly. When I go back to find a verse, I can often find it in an instant—because I carefully marked what was impressive to me.

7. The practice of marking and cross-referencing also yields results in indirect ways. When you take the time, thought, and energy to understand the scriptures by marking and cross-referencing them, you're showing a deep desire to learn, as well as a respect for the word of the Lord. In return, he will bless you in wonderful ways, both directly (in terms of scriptural understanding) and indirectly (in terms of other spiritual gifts).

One Way to Mark Scriptures

There are many ways to mark scriptures. I would like to share with you one way that has worked for me. It's simple— even a child can do it—but of course there are many other ways that are equally valid.

If I were reading 1 Nephi 15:23–24, I might mark the words that are underlined in the example below. Rather than mark a whole verse, I like to highlight certain key words.

1 Nephi 15:23–24

23 And they said unto me: What meaneth the ᵃ<u>rod of iron</u> which our father saw, that led to the tree?

24 And I said unto them that it was the ᵃ<u>word of God</u>; and whoso would hearken unto the word of God, and would ᵇ<u>hold fast</u> unto it, they would <u>never perish</u>; neither could the ᶜ<u>temptations</u> and the fiery ᵈdarts of the

ᶜadversary <u>overpower</u> them unto blindness, to <u>lead them away</u> to destruction.

When I come back to that verse later, I can easily pick up the meaning. I can see that the verse is about the rod of iron, which is the word of God. If you'll hold fast to it, you'll never perish. Temptation will never be able to overpower you or lead you away.

Using Brackets and Numbered Lists

Two other methods of marking I use are called "brackets and numbered lists." As an example, let me refer you to Alma 37:1–10, a sequence of ten verses about the scriptures. You could shade in all ten verses, but that much shading might be overdoing it. Instead, I have found it helpful to put a big opening bracket around the first verse and then a closing bracket around the last verse, when Alma stops talking about that theme. Then, when I open to that page in the future, I immediately know those verses are essentially all about one theme, and I can remind myself at a glance what it's about. Some people would take it a step further and write a key word at the top or in the margin, such as *Scriptures.*

In verse 8 I have used a second method of marking—the numbered lists we talked about in the previous chapter. That verse gives us three things the scriptures will do for us: enlarge the memory of the people, convince us of the error of our ways, and bring us to the knowledge of our God. In the margin near each one I put a number to help me remember that the Lord gives us a list there.

Here is an abbreviated example of "brackets and numbered lists":

Alma 37:1–10

⌈ 1 And now, my son Helaman, I command you that ye⌉
take the ᵃrecords which have been ᵇentrusted with me; . . .
1   8 And now, it has hitherto been wisdom in God that
2 these things should be preserved; for behold, ᵃthey have
3 ᵇenlarged the memory of this people, yea, and convinced
   many of the error of their ways, and brought them to the
   ᶜknowledge of their God unto the salvation of their souls.
     10 And who knoweth but what they will be the ᵃmeans
   of bringing many thousands of them, yea, and also many
   thousands of our ᵇstiffnecked brethren, the Nephites, who
   are now hardening their hearts in sin and iniquities, to the
   ⌊knowledge of their Redeemer?   ⌋

A Simple Approach to Cross-Referencing

Some people are intimidated by the idea of cross-
referencing—they think it looks too hard. But there is a very
simple way to do it.

Let's assume that I read 1 Nephi 15:24 (quoted above) and
was impressed with the phrase "the word of God." Later, as I
read 2 Nephi 32:3, I find the expression "the words of Christ." I
remember having marked something about the word of God
earlier, so I go back and find it in 1 Nephi 15. At that point I
would mark both verses as shown below.

1 Nephi 15:23–24   2N32:3

     23 And they said unto me: What meaneth the ᵃrod of iron
   which our father saw, that led to the tree?
     24 And I said unto them that it was the ᵃword of God;
   and whoso would hearken unto the word of God, and
   would ᵇhold fast unto it, they would never perish; neither
   could the ᶜtemptations and the fiery ᵈdarts of the ᵉadver-
   sary overpower them unto blindness, to lead them away
   to destruction.

2 Nephi 32:3 ———————————1N15:24

3 ªAngels speak by the power of the Holy Ghost; wherefore, they speak the words of Christ. Wherefore, I said
unto you, ᵇfeast upon the ᶜwords of Christ; for behold, the
words of Christ will ᵈtell you all things what ye should do.

Later, as I read on through the book, I find two other scriptures, both in Helaman, that relate to the word of God, and I
add them to my string, as shown:

2 Nephi 32:3 ———————1N15:24; Hel3:29

3 ªAngels speak by the power of the Holy Ghost; wherefore, they speak the words of Christ. Wherefore, I said
unto you, ᵇfeast upon the ᶜwords of Christ; for behold, the
words of Christ will ᵈtell you all things what ye should do.

Helaman 3:29–30 ———————2N32:3; Hel15:7

29 Yea, we see that whosoever will may lay hold upon
the ªword of God, which is ᵇquick and powerful, which
shall ᶜdivide asunder all the cunning and the snares and
the wiles of the devil, and lead the man of Christ in a strait
and ᵈnarrow course across that everlasting ᵉgulf of misery
which is prepared to engulf the wicked—

30 And land their souls, yea, their immortal souls, at the
ªright hand of God in the kingdom of heaven, to sit down
with Abraham, and Isaac, and with Jacob, and with all our
holy fathers, to go no more out.

As you do this, be sure you use some standard and simple
abbreviations for the names of the books. You may want to use
the abbreviations noted in the contents listing of the LDS
edition of the Bible, as well as those additional ones on the back
of that page. (The same list is provided on the second page of
the Triple Combination, right next to the copyright page. Please
note that all references to these scriptures, and to footnotes and
other aids in this chapter, are to the 1979 edition of the Bible and

the 1981 edition of the Triple Combination, both published by
The Church of Jesus Christ of Latter-day Saints.) Or you may
want to shorten your abbreviations even more, to save space—
but be sure you don't confuse Moroni and Mormon by using
the abbreviation "Mor.," or Philemon and Philippians by using
"Phil.," or Moses and Mosiah by using "Mos."

USING THE FOOTNOTES

There is another very important way to find cross-
references. Check the footnotes! For example, if I were reading 1
Nephi 15:24, I might see the superscript *d* right in front of the
word *darts*.

1 Nephi 15:24

24 And I said unto them that it was the *word of God;
and whoso would hearken unto the word of God, and
would *hold fast unto it, they would never perish; neither
could the *temptations and the fiery *darts of the *adversary overpower them unto blindness, to lead them away
to destruction.

If I glanced down at the footnotes, under 24d, I would see
other scriptures I could look up—Eph. 6:16; D&C 3:8; 27:17.
Note that at footnote *d*, verse 24 speaks of "the fiery darts of the
adversary" being unable to "overpower them" and "lead them
away to destruction." When I look up those cross-references,
here is what I find:

Ephesians 6:16

16 Above all, taking the shield of *faith, wherewith ye
shall be able to quench all the fiery *darts of the wicked.

Doctrine and Covenants 3:8

8 Yet you should have been faithful; and he would have
extended his arm and *supported you against all the fiery

*b*darts of the *c*adversary; and he would have been with you in every time of *d*trouble.

Doctrine and Covenants 27:17

17 Taking the shield of faith wherewith ye shall be able to quench all the *a*fiery darts of the wicked.

When I find gems such as these in the footnotes, I mark the superscript letter in the text, then mark the item in the footnote I want to be able to find and remember.

Here is another example of the value of using footnotes, from Doctrine and Covenants 110:12:

12 After this, *a*Elias appeared, and committed the *b*dispensation of the *c*gospel of Abraham . . .

Footnote *a* just before the word *Elias* refers to Doctrine and Covenants 77:9. When we turn to that scripture we learn exactly who this Elias was and what he was doing:

9 Q. What are we to understand by the angel *a*ascending from the east, Revelation 7th chapter and 2nd verse?

A. We are to understand that the angel ascending from the east is he to whom is given the seal of the living God over the twelve tribes of *b*Israel; wherefore, he crieth unto the four angels having the everlasting gospel, saying: Hurt not the earth, neither the sea, nor the trees, till we have sealed the servants of our God in their *c*foreheads. And, if you will receive it, this is *d*Elias which was to come to gather together the tribes of Israel and *e*restore all things.

Superscripts and footnotes will also show you corrections Joseph Smith made in the Bible when he did his inspired translation. Let's look at Exodus 6:3:

3 And I *a*appeared unto *b*Abraham, unto Isaac, *c*and unto Jacob, by *the name of* God Almighty, but by my *d*name JEHOVAH was I not known to them.

This leads us to conclude what the Protestant world and the Catholic world have concluded—that no one knew the name of Jehovah until that time. Yet in the Pearl of Great Price, we learn that Abraham knew about Jehovah, by name, well before Moses' time. (See Abr. 1:16.) Which is right? Do we have an error somehow?

The superscripts and footnotes will give us the answer. If you will refer to the little *c* above the word *and*, it will trigger you to look at the bottom of the page under 3c, where we have an excerpt from the Joseph Smith translation. There we read the correct version of this account, " . . . and unto Jacob. I am the Lord, God Almighty, the Lord JEHOVAH, and was not my name known unto them?" We see then that someone, at some point, basically left a question mark out, and that changed the meaning of the verse.

The footnotes in the Bible also sometimes give another Greek or Hebrew translation of a particular word, yielding a much deeper understanding of what the word means. For example, we read in Matthew 1:16:

> 16 And Jacob begat ªJoseph the husband of ᵇMary, of whom was born ᶜJesus, ᵈwho is called ᵉChrist.

If you see the superscript *e* before the word *Christ*, then look at footnote 16e, you will read, "The Greek title 'Christ' and the Hebrew title 'Messiah' are synonymous, meaning 'Anointed One.'"

Many people have wondered what the difference is between the titles *Christ* and *Messiah*. The answer is as simple as this: The prophets in the Old Testament used the name *Messiah* because they spoke Hebrew. And the prophets and apostles in the New Testament used the name *Christ* because it was written in Greek. If you know that, you'll have a greater understanding as you're reading.

Many of these insights will pass us by if we don't look at

the footnotes. But sometimes we forget to look at the bottom of the page to see what's there. Here is a simple way to remind yourself: Take some time to go through all your scriptures, quickly glancing over the footnotes at the bottom of each page. When you find one that gives an interpretation or added meaning, put a red mark on it; then put a mark on the corresponding superscript on the verse above it. This approach takes an initial investment of time, but the exercise will benefit you in your reading for years to come.

When I highlight items in my scriptures, I like to use a red pencil—it stands out and doesn't "bleed" through the page. When I'm actually writing in the margins—notes or cross-references—I use a black marking pen. It matches the print and looks nice. But some people use varying colors and like the results. Choose a method that suits your style and personality.

A PERSONAL EXPERIENCE WITH FOOTNOTES

Once two or three years ago my family had an experience with using footnotes that was a real blessing to us—and it reinforced some of the approaches we have been talking about in this chapter.

We were reading in Mosiah 3:15, which says, "many signs, and wonders, and types, and shadows showed he unto them, concerning his coming."

We stopped there and asked, what does "types and shadows" mean? My wife and I tried to explain that a type and shadow is like a symbol; it is an example, often in life, of something that stands for something else. For example, the ancient Israelites sacrificed lambs unto God, and that is a type and shadow of Jesus (who is called the Lamb of God) being sacrificed for our sins.

We asked our children to help us think of all the types and shadows of Christ that we could. Without referring to any sources, we were able to compile a list of a dozen or so. Even our daughter who was seven at the time was able to help. "The bread we take in sacrament meeting is an example of Jesus' flesh," she said. "Isn't that one of them?" Of course, she was right. It is a beautiful type of Christ.

Another example is the water in the sacrament. Also, when you're baptized you're immersed in the water, symbolizing the death of man and of Christ, and then you're raised out of the water, symbolizing the resurrection.

When we ran out of ideas on our own, we turned to the Topical Guide and Bible Dictionary. The superscript in the verse told us where to look in the Topical Guide—under "Jesus Christ, Types of, in Anticipation; Passover; Symbolism."

For several mornings we searched through the Topical Guide and Bible Dictionary, looking up scriptures we thought would give us more insight into types and shadows of Jesus Christ. It was a wonderful experience, a learning experience not only about types and shadows but also about how the scriptures and scriptural helps work.

OTHER STUDY AIDS

There are a few other scriptural aids I would recommend you become familiar with—they will enhance your study of the word of God.

• Chapter headings. The headings in the chapters to the LDS editions of the scriptures have been carefully written and reviewed. One benefit of these headings is that they give us a focus before we start reading, and thus they can generate additional questions in our minds before we read.

• The index in the Triple Combination. This index has some very valuable references that are not found in the Topical Guide.

• The maps in the Triple Combination. In the back of the

Doctrine and Covenants are four maps that help us to understand the geographical context of the revelations in our dispensation.

• The Topical Guide, which is in the back of the Bible. We have touched on this, but it deserves another mention. This guide gives us hundreds of scriptural topics, arranged alphabetically, to help in the study of the scriptures. Entries begin with *Aaron* and go to *Zipporah.*

• The Bible Dictionary, also in the back of the Bible. This is an alphabetical listing of many of the key persons, places, and concepts in the Bible, with discussions on each. The dictionary also includes a helpful chart on the chronology of the Bible and a harmony of the four Gospels.

• The Joseph Smith Translation. Again, we have touched on this, but I want to reemphasize that there are scores of helpful quotations from the Joseph Smith Translation in the footnotes to the Bible; in addition, there is a section of longer quotations in the back of the Bible. (You'll find it just before the gazetteer that goes with the maps.)

• The maps in the back of the Bible. There are twenty-two maps (with a gazetteer) of such things as "the ancient world at the time of the Patriarchs," "the empire of David and Solomon," "the Persian empire," "Jesus' Galilean ministry," and "Paul's Journey to Rome."

• The computerized scriptures. If you have a computer, you might want to consider investing in a program that gives you the LDS scriptures in electronic form. Such programs can enable you to search a word or combination of words in the scriptures, and they will give you the result literally in an instant.

Concerning these helps—and the scriptures themselves—President Howard W. Hunter said:

> We ought to have a church full of women and men who know the scriptures thoroughly, who cross-reference and mark them, who develop lessons and talks out of the

Topical Guide, and who have mastered the maps, the Bible Dictionary, and the other helps that are contained in this wonderful set of standard works. . . .

Not in this dispensation, surely not in *any* dispensation, have the scriptures—the enduring, enlightening word of God—been so readily available and so helpfully structured for the use of every man, woman, and child who will search them. The written word of God is in the most readable and accessible form ever provided to lay members in the history of the world. Surely we will be held accountable if we do not read them. (Satellite address to religious educators, 10 Feb. 1989.)

A Note about Verses

When the original manuscript to the Book of Mormon was delivered to the printer, it was all in one paragraph—no chapters and no verses.

Since then the Church has provided both verses and chapters, and I am very grateful for it—they make the book much easier to read, and they give us common reference points, such as Alma 11:4, which we did not have before.

But sometimes we let the verses and chapters indicate our starting and stopping points—and they may not always be the best divisions. We need to look beyond verses and chapters and see the underlying thought.

CHAPTER 9

SEARCH DILIGENTLY: HOW DOES THIS APPLY TO ME?

When I was a young missionary I decided to read the Book of Mormon again. In the very first verse I was touched in my heart as I read, "I, Nephi, having been born of goodly parents . . ."

I began to ponder the meaning of that, asking questions and applying the verse to myself. "What are goodly parents? Have I been born of goodly parents?" From that day until this, when I read those words the testimony comes to me again and again that I, Gene Cook, have been born of goodly parents. Sometimes I have pondered that verse and have felt deeply humbled. I've wept at times as I've thought about how truly blessed I was to have goodly parents to launch me on my way. I could never be doing what I am doing in my life if it were not for them. At those times I have stopped my reading and offered a humble prayer to the Lord, expressing pure gratitude for my family. All these feelings come from reading the first phrase of the first verse of the Book of Mormon and taking it into my heart.

" . . . Therefore I was taught somewhat in all the learning of my father; and having seen many afflictions in the course of my days, nevertheless, having been highly favored of the Lord in all my days . . ."

I read that phrase as a missionary—"highly favored of the Lord"—and I stopped with other questions: "Does the Lord really have favorites? Could that be true? What does it mean?

I thought he loved everybody the same. If Nephi was highly favored, how could I become highly favored? If there is such a thing as being favored of the Lord, that's what I want to be. But how do you do it? How can I apply this passage to myself?

I remember turning from my reading as a missionary and praying, "Father in Heaven, help me understand that. I don't know what it means, that one could apparently be favored over another. I really thought that thou dost love all men the same."

I didn't get an answer immediately, but I did seventeen chapters later. In 1 Nephi 17 the Lord is describing how the people in Moses' time were driven from the land. Then at the end of verse 33 he asked this question: "Do ye suppose that they were righteous? Behold, I say unto you, Nay." They were not. "Do ye suppose our fathers would have been more choice than they if they had been righteous?" Now that's an excellent question, giving a partial answer to what I had asked earlier. But then comes this great truth: "Behold, the Lord esteemeth all flesh in one," meaning, "I love all men the same." But "he that is righteous is favored of God." (See 1 Ne. 17:33–35.)

I remember reading that verse and feeling the Spirit of the Lord rest upon me, bearing testimony, "Elder Cook, there is the answer you sought seventeen chapters ago."

If you want to be favored of the Lord, keep his commandments. Then, by law, you will receive the blessings of the Lord, and you will be more highly favored than someone who is not keeping the commandments. I later discovered that Joseph Smith taught in Lectures on Faith (see lecture 6, paragraph 4) that we could become the very "favorites of heaven," the same concept that I now understood, at least in part.

I give this experience as a simple example of this principle. If we're reading carefully, praying, pondering, asking questions, and trying to apply the scriptures to ourselves, we'll come to marvelous truths. When I read that passage in 1 Nephi 1:1, I felt that I wanted to be one of the favorites of heaven. I wanted to learn and apply that truth in my weak way as a nineteen-year-old young man. And as I prayed, the Lord gave me the answer, telling me what to do.

LIKENING SCRIPTURES TO YOURSELF

A related skill is to liken the verse unto yourself. When we reviewed Ether 12:27 earlier, for example, we saw how much it applied to ourselves.

> And if men come unto me I will show unto them their weakness. I give unto men weakness that they may be humble; and my grace is sufficient for all men that humble themselves before me; for if they humble themselves before me, and have faith in me, then will I make weak things become strong unto them.

To apply this scripture to yourself, you can ask yourself questions such as "Have I come unto the Lord? Has he shown me my weakness? When is it that I am not very humble? Do I understand the grace of Christ? Do I have faith in him? Have I ever experienced the Lord making weak things become strong unto me?"

USING SUBSTITUTION

Another way of applying the verse is to use the principle of substitution. The scriptures are often written in the second person, with the Lord speaking. Change the point of view to first person by reading with your own name in each verse:

> And if Gene Cook will come unto me I will show unto him his weakness. I give unto Gene Cook weakness that he may be humble; and my grace is sufficient for him, even for him, as he humbles himself before me; for if Gene

Cook humbles himself before me, and has faith in me,
then will I make weak things become strong unto him.

There is another way to use this same principle. Try reading the verse in first person:

> And if I come unto Christ he will show unto me my
> weakness. He gives unto me weakness that I may be
> humble; and his grace is sufficient for me if I will humble
> myself before him; for if I humble myself before him, and
> have faith in him, then will he make weak things become
> strong unto me.

TAKING NOTES

There is still more we can do in applying the scriptures to
ourselves. As you read, I would recommend that you have a
piece of paper handy and make notes of the feelings you have.

I might say, "When were some specific times recently when
I didn't feel very humble? When did I try to go off on my own
and not seek to exercise faith and do the Lord's will? What do I
need to do to change, so that I can receive these blessings the
Lord talks about?"

As I ask myself these questions, I will have feelings from
the Spirit, guiding me in the direction I should go. I ought to
make note of my feelings—and of the Spirit's response—so I
can remember and learn better.

I bear witness that if you will humble yourself before the
Lord and pray for his guidance, he will tell you what you need
to know. You will be grateful he has awakened your spirit to
that need in your life, and you will grow accordingly.

Remember, applying what you read to yourself is not only
important in its own right, but it also is a key element of quali-
fying to receive the Lord's voice as you read. As you grow in
your willingness and ability to let the scriptures speak to you,

personally, you will also be growing in your willingness and ability to receive the words of the Lord to you, personally. It is a wonderful cycle of application and understanding that need never end.

CHAPTER 10

OBEY WHAT YOU LEARN
TO RECEIVE MORE

Throughout much of this section we have talked about how we can hear the voice of the Lord through the scriptures. We need to pray in faith, humble ourselves, and follow the steps of searching diligently—pondering, asking questions, discovering patterns, marking and cross-referencing, and applying what we read to ourselves. If we do those things with an honest heart, it is my testimony that we will receive guidance from the Lord.

But that's not all the Lord asks of us. If you want to learn more from the Lord, as a rule you have to be willing to obey the things he has already given you. If you really want to have him communicate with you frequently, if you want to hear his voice, if you want to receive revelation and instruction, you have to obey the voice when it comes.

"THE FIRST LAW OF HEAVEN"

President Joseph F. Smith taught a principle that has often been quoted since: "Obedience is the first law of heaven." (*Journal of Discourses*, 16:247–48.) Obedience not only helps us to be saved in the celestial kingdom of God (see A of F 3), but it also helps us grow in knowledge and understanding. Obedience to the Lord's voice helps us receive additional instructions from that voice.

The Lord clearly taught the importance and blessing of obedience in our day when he said through Joseph Smith,

> If a person gains more knowledge and intelligence in this life through his diligence and obedience than another, he will have so much the advantage in the world to come. (D&C 130:19.)

This tells me that being diligent and obedient increases our knowledge. Perhaps a parallel can be seen in another scripture, where we read that we should "seek learning, even by study and also by faith." (D&C 88:118.)

Could it be that *diligence* and *study* are comparable ways of gaining knowledge? And could it be that *obedience* and *faith* also are parallel to each other?

These scriptures seem to suggest that there are two different paths to learning and that both must always be followed. First, we gain an understanding of what the Lord has said to his children in general by searching the scriptures—by *diligently* reading, by *studying*. Then, having built that foundation, we can begin to grow in our understanding of what he would have us do in our own lives. We do this as we are *obedient* to what we have learned, *obeying* the Lord in *faith*.

This attitude and practice of obedience completes the circle in the pattern of hearing the Lord's voice. Our obedience to his instructions—both general and personalized—qualifies us to receive additional instructions, and thus we continue from truth to truth, learning and doing all that the Lord requires. By this means we grow "line upon line, precept upon precept" (D&C 98:12; also see Isa. 28:10, 13) "unto a perfect man, unto the measure of the stature of the fulness of Christ" (Eph. 4:13).

OBEDIENCE BEGINS WITH REPENTANCE

When one begins to obey, the first requirement is to repent. I recently read a statement that says "You'll know you've learned a lesson when your actions change." If it is the desire of your heart to change, and if you are seeking and trying diligently to change, the Lord will acknowledge your desires and your efforts. He will give you added understanding of what you need to do. The more quickly you obey, the more quickly you will receive added instruction. Very simply, if you will repent and change, you'll receive more light.

For example, let's assume I am reading a passage about being more humble. As I ponder the passage, a feeling begins to grow in me—was I a little prideful about the response I received after giving a talk last week? Later, as I pray, the Lord speaks to me through the Spirit and says, "You're right in your feelings. You weren't humble enough about that talk."

"I DON'T HAVE AS MANY PROBLEMS . . ."

The Testimony of a Young Man

"Reading the Book of Mormon was a challenge. Our family hasn't quite read all the Book of Mormon, but we have made a goal to read all of it by the end of this year.

"We read the scriptures right before school starts. I think it helps me a lot because I don't have as many problems thinking about bad things as I did before we started reading. We had been reading off and on before, but when we heard the bishop's challenge, we went for it.

"The scriptures really make me think about what hardships prophets went through back then."

I resolve to work on that harder. I think, "I've made good progress, and I want to make even more. Next time I give a talk I'll be careful that I don't take credit to myself."

But what I don't realize in this process is that perhaps pride has also become manifest in the way I have been treating my wife and my children. It has reached into my work, into my Church calling, and into other aspects of my life.

If I will truly seek the Lord's guidance in my life, looking humbly and honestly at myself as the Spirit teaches me the truth, I will learn that my pride goes deeper than the issue of giving talks. I will know that I've got to seek to get pride out of all the facets of my life—that is the only way I can begin to repent in order to obey the truth. That will take a bit of work, and it will probably take many months, or maybe even many years, to totally eliminate that particular spiritual weakness.

The Lord does not require that we become perfect before he will bless us. But he does desire that we recognize the truth and seek the best we can to begin the effort to change.

ESTEEM THE LORD'S TRUTHS

A second element of obedience is to esteem the truths we are given, valuing them as of great worth to us.

Imagine how the Lord feels when he gives us a revelation and we respond by taking it lightly, soon forgetting it and not letting it have any impact on our lives. When we fail to hold his truths precious and to obey what the Lord says, we often close the door to further direction—until we repent.

On the other hand, if we try to show him and ourselves that we value the great truth he gives us—we learn it, we assimilate it into our lives, we take it into our own hearts—he continues to give revelation.

Here are a few suggestions of ways we can show the Lord

that we esteem his truths. We have talked about these concepts earlier, but let's take a look at them in this context now.

We can ponder a truth in all facets of our lives. Many times the Lord will reveal a problem in a given area of your life, and if you're not careful, you'll think you now understand the whole problem. Yet that problem may be permeating your life and actions in many other ways. We saw an example of this before—how a person can become prideful in giving talks and not know that that pride has permeated his life and many of his relationships.

Pondering is often a prelude to understanding. When Jesus visited the Nephites, he asked the people to return to their homes "and ponder upon the things which I have said, and ask of the Father, in my name, that ye may understand." (3 Ne. 17:3.) Moroni prefaced his invitation to ask concerning the truthfulness of the Book of Mormon with an instruction for us to "ponder it in your hearts." (Moro. 10:3.) Joseph F. Smith "sat in [his] room pondering over the scriptures" when he received his marvelous vision of the redemption of the dead. (D&C 138:1.)

Certainly as we ponder the things we read in the scriptures we will gain great insights into how they apply to us.

We can record what the Lord gives to us. As you read the scriptures, make a note of the ideas, feelings, impressions, and understandings you receive. I always read with a pad of paper or a Dictaphone nearby. When I find a great truth, I either take the time to write it down or I dictate my thoughts and feelings onto a tape. That way I can show the Lord that I esteem his words, and I can be sure not to lose what I have been given.

Over the years my notes have proven to be of great value to me. I can go back on later occasions and read them (they're now on computer) until they're in my heart, and I can obey better.

I had a wonderful experience with receiving—and recording—instructions from the Lord once as I waited for a flight in a Bolivian airport. I was exhausted and welcomed the opportunity to get some rest in the airport. But as I was drifting off to sleep, I had a very strong feeling that I should awaken and write down some ideas. The desire to sleep was insistent, but the promptings of the Spirit were even more powerful. I did write; in fact, I wrote for nearly three hours, receiving solutions

"THE BEST BOOK I HAVE EVER READ"
The Testimony of a Young Woman

"I am a young woman seventeen years old, and I decided to take on the challenge to read the Book of Mormon. I started in December and ended on February 23. This was a first experience for me and I plan for it to be a beginning of many more. Reading the Book of Mormon was so exciting. I have always thought of it as some neat scripture. Now it is the best book I have ever read. The Church of Jesus Christ of Latter-day Saints is the one and only true church. Living by Church standards has helped me a lot.

"The people in the Book of Mormon are such amazing people. We have always forgotten what God does for us and turn to evil. But Heavenly Father always puts his loving arms around us and helps us make things better again. By reading the Book of Mormon daily, I have learned what is left for me to do. I have never felt a greater anticipation before as I have felt with this reading. I couldn't wait to do my homework so that I could read it. I hope that inside this letter you have felt a little of the love I have for the restoration of the true Church, for you, for the prophet, and most importantly, for my dear Heavenly Father."

to some organizational problems I had struggled with for years. I felt a great outpouring of the Spirit that day, and I excitedly wrote down each inspired thought.

I believe that experience came because I had been diligent in searching the scriptures. And I believe the experience continued for the greater part of three hours because I "esteemed greatly" that which the Lord was giving to me, recording it and holding it as something of true value.

We can use the powerful tool of memorizing scriptures. We have had a fun time with that in our family—frequently we will pick some key verses and memorize them together.

I have discovered that many times you don't fully understand a scripture until you memorize it. And sometimes I have memorized a passage because it seemed important and valuable to me—then afterwards I discovered deeper meanings that I hadn't even known were there.

When you find a passage that particularly impresses you, consider taking the time to commit it to memory, word perfect. Then not only will you be able to remember it, but you will probably grow in your understanding as well.

But that's not all. By memorizing scripture you show the Lord that you esteem his words to be of great value—and then he will be more likely to speak to you and give you more.

President Spencer W. Kimball began this practice when he was a nine-year-old boy. He milked cows every day and said to himself, "What a waste of time, to sit on a three-legged stool. Maybe there is something else I could do while I am milking." So he began to sing the songs of Zion to himself. Then he "got a copy of the Articles of Faith and put it on the ground right beside me and I went through them, over and over again, a thousand times." Next, he typed a copy of the Ten Commandments and memorized them. Finally, as he grew a little older, "I typed scriptures that I thought would be helpful to me, and I learned them. . . . If every Latter-day Saint would do this, I think it would be a wonderful thing." (*The Teachings of Spencer W. Kimball*, ed. Edward L. Kimball [Salt Lake City: Bookcraft, 1982], 131.)

President Gordon B. Hinckley has made a similar suggestion: "May I suggest that in our family night gatherings we make it a project to memorize one scripture citation a week pertinent to this work," he said. "At the conclusion of a year our children will have on their lips a fund of scripture which will remain with them throughout their lives." (Conference Report, Apr. 1959, 120.)

We can do our best to share with others. If you don't understand something well enough to verbalize it to someone else, it may not be your truth yet. On the other hand, if you want to grow in your understanding of a truth, try to explain it to someone else.

As far as it is appropriate, then, do your best to share your testimony with someone else, to bear witness of the majesty of the Lord's teachings to you. If you will do that by the power of the Spirit, you will be a much more powerful teacher and you will reach the hearts of those you love. You will also receive more of the Lord's word to you, to guide you and help you in your life—and to help you be a more inspired aid to others.

I am grateful for this testimony from Brigham Young:

> A man who wishes to receive light and knowledge, to increase in the faith of the Holy Gospel, and to grow in the knowledge of the truth as it is in Jesus Christ, will find that when he imparts knowledge to others he will also grow and increase. Be not miserly in your feelings, but get knowledge and understanding by freely imparting it to others, and be not like a man who selfishly hoards his gold; for that man will not thus increase upon the amount, but will become contracted in his views and feelings. So the man who will not impart freely of the knowledge he has received will become so contracted in his mind that he cannot receive truth when it is presented to him. Wherever you see an opportunity to do good, do it, for that is the

way to increase and grow in the knowledge of the truth. (*Deseret Weekly*, 9 May 1855, 68.)

Of course, we need to remind ourselves that at times the Lord gives us sacred truths that ought not to be shared. If we were to do so, the Spirit would be offended. The Holy Ghost will tell us the difference so we will know when and if we should share.

THE LORD'S BLESSING OF GUIDANCE

We have spent considerable time and space over many chapters discussing how we can hear the voice of the Lord through the scriptures. (A summary of the pattern is provided on the previous page.) Remember, that is one of the primary reasons why we read scripture—not just to learn doctrine, though that is important; not just to be able to give lessons, though that is needful—but to be able to receive personal revelation from our Heavenly Father. By reading scripture we can draw closer to him, receive his voice, and know the course we need to take to be able to return to him again.

As President Spencer W. Kimball said, if we will be "determined and conscientious" in our search of the scriptures, "we shall indeed find answers to our problems and peace in our hearts." This, of course, comes as we hear the voice of the Lord in our reading. President Kimball continues: "We shall experience the Holy Ghost broadening our understanding, find new insights, witness an unfolding pattern of all scripture; and the doctrines of the Lord shall come to have more meaning to us than we ever thought possible. As a consequence, we shall have greater wisdom with which to guide ourselves and our families." (*The Teachings of Spencer W. Kimball*, ed. Edward L. Kimball [Salt Lake City: Bookcraft, 1982], 135.)

What a blessing from our Father in Heaven! He gives us all we need to be able to proceed through our days in this life, guided by the precious gift of the Holy Ghost and the powerful tool of the scriptures. What a wonderful, loving Father we have! Every day I am filled with gratitude for these blessings—and I am sure you are, too.

LEARNING TO HEAR THE VOICE OF THE LORD

A Suggested Pattern

Here is a summary of the pattern discussed in the previous chapters:

1. Pray in faith
2. Humble yourself
3. Search diligently
   A. Ponder
   B. Ask questions
   C. Discover patterns
   D. Mark and cross-reference
   E. Apply to self
4. Obey truths learned
   A. Repent, change (then receive more light)
   B. Esteem truths to be of "great worth" by:
      —Pondering and applying to all facets of life
      —Recording
      —Memorizing
      —Sharing

You will then have heard the voice of the Lord to you and will begin to experience the "mighty change in your heart." (Alma 5:14.)

SIX SUGGESTIONS FOR A RICHER READING EXPERIENCE

As we conclude this section, I would like to make six final suggestions about how we all can have a richer experience with the scriptures.

First, I would suggest that we ought to be studying the scriptures every day, and we ought to be praying as we read. Our latter-day prophets have taught that being born again is a daily process, and that the way to seek that blessing is through daily prayer and daily scripture study. Let us be faithful in not allowing the devil, who is so quick to put up obstacles and give us diversions, to entice us into failing to spend our time with the words of the Lord. Satan knows what will happen if you don't, and he knows what will happen if you do. He will do all in his power to keep you from reading in the scriptures. Don't let him succeed.

Second, let us study daily with our spouse or family members. Missionaries ought to be studying with their companions. Single people might study with a friend whenever possible. It takes added humility to study with someone else—that's one main reason why many of us don't do it—but we will often learn more when studying with someone else than by ourselves. Why? Because we can teach one another, sharing both testimony and insight.

Third, remember that the scriptures are for all people. As the Lord said through Nephi:

118

Know ye not that I, the Lord your God, have created all men, and that I remember those who are upon the isles of the sea; and that I rule in the heavens above and in the earth beneath; and I bring forth my word unto the children of men, yea, even upon all the nations of the earth? (2 Ne. 29:7.)

None is excepted; the Lord's word is for all.

Some Latter-day Saints say, "I just don't understand what the scriptures say." I truly believe that such people have forgotten to humble themselves and to pray before they read. The Lord's promise is that his holy word was given to all—even you—yet we must follow the process the Lord has prescribed. If you're not sure you can remember the other things we talk about in this book, don't worry about it. Just remember this: be humble and prayerful. Even children can do that. Be careful not to make it more complicated or difficult than it is.

Fourth, remember to stay focused on the most important reason the Lord invites us to study the scriptures. That reason is to receive direction from heaven and to hear the Lord's voice speaking to us, as individuals. Don't get overwhelmed with the ideas I have shared with you about patterns or cross-referencing or anything else. These are helpful skills and tools—I hope you will use them, and I hope they will be a blessing to you. But they are only means to an end, which end is to hear the voice of the Lord.

The coming of that voice may be as simple as a quiet moment when the Lord breathes peace into your heart, and you know, because of his witness, that he loves you. Or you may feel gentle stirrings to change something in your life. If you can receive those blessings, don't be too worried about these other things.

Fifth, I have found it to be of great benefit in my life, a few times a year, to seek to have a "general spiritual checkup" and find out my standing with the Lord. I like to check in with the Lord and ask, "Where am I? What ought I to be doing? Heavenly Father, dost thou have some direction for me in my calling that I am not now aware of? What is the most dominant need in my family? Help me." If you will do that, prayerfully asking for help, seeking to reestablish your bearings in life, and pondering the scriptures with those questions in mind, I bear testimony that the Lord will give you answers. Many of them will come directly through prayer, while many others will come as you read and ponder the scriptures. Through those two means, the Lord will speak to your heart, writing his will upon your soul, and you will come to understandings you did not have before.

Sixth, believe that as you do these things consistently, you will experience a miracle in your life. The scriptures will combine with your humility and your prayers to bring about the mighty change of converting you to God, with an unshakable testimony in the Lord.

I have always loved these words of Nephi:

> I said unto them that it was the word of God [meaning the rod of iron]; and whoso would hearken unto the word of God, and would hold fast unto it, they would never perish; neither could the temptations and the fiery darts of the adversary overpower them unto blindness, to lead them away to destruction. (1 Ne. 15:24.)

What a tremendous promise! If we will bring the Lord's words into our lives, we will never fall away. We will be held firm in the faith and will never perish.

Here is another beautiful promise, this one from Helaman:

> We see that whosoever will [you have to be willing] may lay hold upon the word of God, which is quick and powerful, which shall divide asunder all the cunning and the snares and the wiles of the devil, and lead the man of Christ in a strait and narrow course across that everlasting gulf of misery which is prepared to engulf the wicked—
>
> And land their souls, yea, their immortal souls, at the

right hand of God in the kingdom of heaven, to sit down with Abraham, and Isaac, and with Jacob, and with all our holy fathers, to go no more out. (Hel. 3:29–30.)

If we will hold firmly to the words of the Lord, we're assured that we'll be unshakable in the faith, and we'll be blessed to enter into the celestial kingdom.

HOW WILL I KNOW HOW I AM DOING IN SCRIPTURE READING?

Is there a way to know if we are doing well or poorly in our scripture reading? Has Heavenly Father given us any guides to help us know if we are pleasing him? The answer to both questions is "Yes," and the keys to the answer are found in the scriptures. Here are some spiritual tests that will help (note that each one has much to do with our hearts and our minds).

One scripture that helps me know how I am doing is found in the Doctrine and Covenants. The Lord said,

> These words are not of men nor of man, . . .
> For it is my voice which speaketh them unto you; . . .
> Wherefore, you can testify that you have heard my voice, and know my words. (D&C 18:34–36.)

I bear testimony that you have heard the voice of the Lord if you have received the words of scripture in your heart. You have heard his voice if you receive revelation, impressions, thoughts, feelings, and ideas from the Spirit, both when you're reading scripture and when you're engaged in other pursuits. Receiving the Lord's voice consistently is one measure of how well you are doing in scripture reading.

The Lord gave us a related test in the book of Luke. After Jesus was resurrected but before he would shown himself to the Apostles, he was walking on the road to Emmaus with two disciples, but they didn't know who he was. They stopped at an inn together, and he broke bread for them and blessed it, and then he disappeared from their sight.

After he was gone, they commented to one another that they should have recognized him, for the Lord had given them spiritual clues.

"Did not our heart burn within us, while he talked with us by the way," they asked one another, "and while he opened to us the scriptures?" (Luke 24:32.)

This is another test we can make as we look into our hearts. We can ask ourselves: "When I read the scriptures, does my heart burn within me? Does my heart burn as I bear testimony of the scriptures, and as I use their stories and examples?" If your answer is yes, you have another indicator that you are doing well.

A third scripture that gives me a key is again found in the Doctrine and Covenants. Section 35, verse 20, gives us an answer to an important question, but we need to supply the question. Here is how I would phrase it: Where does the Lord keep his scriptures?

The Lord's answer: "The scriptures shall be given, even as they are in mine own bosom, to the salvation of mine own elect." The Lord has his scriptures in his own bosom, as it were, deep in his own heart. The challenge is for us to get them there as well, to live the words, to teach the words, to have them burning in our hearts. As we do that, they will be in our bosoms. Then, when we stand up to speak and testify, we will speak the words of the Lord through his Spirit, as does the Lord himself.

The last scripture that helps me know how I'm doing is in the writings of Paul:

> For who hath known the mind of the Lord, that he may instruct him? But we have the mind of Christ. (1 Cor. 2:16.)

Since the scriptures come from the mind of Christ, they help us to have the Spirit, which brings us to a oneness of mind and heart with the Lord. Therefore, as you read and study and assimilate the words of the Lord through the scriptures, you are in the process of absorbing the mind of Christ. You begin to think as he thinks. You begin to feel as he feels. You begin to speak as he speaks.

How can we know how well we are doing in our scripture reading? We can know we are doing well when we hear his voice (both in the scriptures directly and through revelation), when our hearts burn within us at hearing his word, when we receive the words of Christ into our bosoms, and when we receive them into our minds (and thus we learn how to feel as he feels and think as he thinks.)

THREE TESTIMONIES

As we conclude this section, I would like to share with you three testimonies—one from a man who recounts a sweet experience with scripture reading, another from Parley P. Pratt, and finally my own.

"Every Page Testified of My Savior"

Our stake president recently gave my wife and me counsel to listen to a set of cassette tapes given by a General Authority on personal and family scripture study. We took the opportunity of a trip to the Oregon coast during the winter time to snuggle in beside a warm fire and listen to the instruction. The Spirit was very strong and we received personal revelation that our long-time tradition of reading the scriptures together daily would be an even greater blessing if we really *studied* them.

On a recent business trip the witness of that revelation manifest itself in the most wonderful manner. I often read the scriptures as I travel. Since my territory is the east coast and I live in Washington state, I have many hours of free time to read on each trip. On this particular trip, instead of just reading the Book of Mormon, I read it with a significant purpose. I took a new missionary copy of the Book of Mormon and my red pencil and began reading it with the express purpose of finding what it could teach me of Jesus Christ. All the way to the east coast I read and underlined, and then again all the way home.

I cannot express the feelings that grew within me as I read. Each page taught me more of my Lord and my God. It seemed as though virtually every page testified of my Savior, my Redeemer, the Lamb of God. I came to understand, through the testimony of the Spirit, that each name given him teaches something of the wonder of who Jesus Christ is: Son of God, Son of Righteousness, the Only Begotten of the Father; Maker, Creator, Lord of Hosts, the God of Nature; King of the Earth, King of Heaven, King of kings; God of Israel, the Holy One of Jacob, and Redeemer of Israel.

With my greatly deepened testimony of who He is also came a broadening depth of understanding of the wonder of his personality. Merciful, deliverer, giver of hope, Redeemer, loving, kind, friend, Father. I found other names given him, many others. I felt as if my heart would burst, for it could not contain the feelings within—feelings of testimony that seemed to be inextricably connected to each name given to my Savior.

Since my conversion in Vietnam some twenty-five years ago I have always had a strong testimony of the Prophet Joseph Smith. I have loved him to the degree that I think I have felt like Brigham Young when he said, "I feel to shout Hallelujah every day to think that I ever knew the Prophet Joseph Smith." Though I have not come to know him personally like Brigham Young was blessed to know him, I have come to know him through the Spirit in a very profound way. Joseph has always seemed to be my brother and my friend.

But the Savior has always seemed to be too perfect for me to comprehend—too much beyond my reach.

I have read the New Testament and the Book of Mormon many times and have learned much about him. I think I have had a good understanding of the doctrine of the atonement. On occasion over the years, I have felt the sweet spirit of the forgiveness of my sins. I have been blessed with many spiritual witnesses of the gospel and a strong testimony of its truth.

But in all this, I have not known my Savior—at least in the sense that I knew I needed to know him.

After the experience I had on that trip, I now have a personal testimony of Jesus Christ—and it is growing. There are times when I can barely speak his name, I am so moved with feelings of love for him. My prayers now often reach out for a day when I shall enjoy his company, when I shall be worthy to be his friend.

I hope we will gain the following lessons from this account:

• This good brother renewed his desire to *study* the scriptures and not just to read them.

• He began to read the Book of Mormon with a particular purpose—to learn more about Jesus Christ.

• He received feelings and understandings from the Spirit about our Savior.

• The combination of scripture study and prayer has given him a choice and deep testimony of Jesus Christ—and a newly strengthened desire to be with him.

"I Preferred Reading to Sleep":
An Experience of Parley P. Pratt

Parley P. Pratt had a remarkable experience in coming to a knowledge of the gospel of Jesus Christ and a testimony of the Book of Mormon. Here is his account in his own words:

> We visited an old Baptist deacon by the name of Hamlin. After hearing of our appointment for the evening, he began to tell of a book, a STRANGE BOOK, a VERY STRANGE BOOK! in his possession, which had been just published. This book, he said, purported to have been originally written on plates either of gold or brass, by a branch of the tribes of Israel; and to have been discovered and translated by a young man near Palmyra, in the State of New York, by the aid of visions, or the ministry of angels. I inquired of him how or where the book was to be obtained. He promised me the perusal of it, at his house the next day, if I would call. I felt a strange interest in the book. . . . Next morning I called at his house, where, for the first time, my eyes beheld the "BOOK OF MORMON"—that book of books—that record which reveals the antiquities of the "New World" back to the remotest ages, and which unfolds the destiny of its people and the world for all time to come;—that Book which contains the fulness of the gospel of a crucified and risen Redeemer;—that Book which reveals a lost remnant of Joseph, and which was the principal means, in the hands of God, of directing the entire course of my future life.
>
> I opened it with eagerness, and read its title page. I then read the testimony of several witnesses in relation to the manner of its being found and translated. After this I commenced its contents by course. I read all day; eating was a burden, I had no desire for food; sleep was a burden when the night came, for I preferred reading to sleep.
>
> As I read, the spirit of the Lord was upon me, and I knew and comprehended that the book was true, as plainly and manifestly as a man comprehends and knows that he exists. My joy was now full, as it were, and I

rejoiced sufficiently to more than pay me for all the sorrows, sacrifices and toils of my life. . . .

I esteemed the Book, or the information contained in it, more than all the riches of the world. Yes; I verily believe that I would not at that time have exchanged the knowledge I then possessed, for a legal title to all the beautiful farms, houses, villages and property which passed in review before me, on my journey through one of the most flourishing settlements of western New York. (*Autobiography of Parley P. Pratt* [Salt Lake City: Deseret Book Co., 1985], 18, 20, 22.)

What a wonderful account of discovering the Book of Mormon! Note that the book had such an influence on Elder Pratt that it "was the principal means, in the hands of God, of directing the entire course of my future life." We should all seek to be so influenced by the Lord and by his word!

Here are a few other important points from this account:

• He approached the scriptures with "eagerness."

• He was so desirous of receiving the Lord's word as found in the Book of Mormon that "I read all day; eating was a burden, I had no desire for food; sleep was a burden."

• As he read, he received the Spirit of the Lord, "and I knew and comprehended that the book was true."

• His testimony of the Book of Mormon was as strong as his testimony that he himself existed.

• He "esteemed" the book as of great worth—"more than all the riches of the world."

"I Bear Witness":
My Testimony of Personal Scripture Reading

I bear witness that the scriptures change men's lives, just as in these accounts we have just reviewed.

I bear witness that two things have helped me more in my

life than any other single thing I know of—prayer and scripture reading.

I bear testimony of the importance of our truly searching the words of the Lord, of learning how to search humbly, and of treating the scriptures in such a way that they will speak to us through revelation from the Lord himself.

I pray the Lord will bless you as you go forward now, seeking and searching more intently on your own. I remind you once again that the only thing you really have to learn is to truly pray and humble yourself, and the Lord will lead you, teach you, and bring you to him.

I bear testimony that these things are true, and declare in solemnity, and in the name of the Lord Jesus Christ, that the scriptures are the words of God himself, one of his most priceless gifts to us, his children.

FAMILY STUDY

BLESSING YOUR FAMILY WITH THE WORD OF THE LORD

HOW WILL STUDYING
TOGETHER BLESS MY FAMILY?

Some years ago, a parent shared with me a wonderful experience he had with his nine-year-old son, Scott. Scott had been asked to give a talk in Primary. "We had tried to teach our children that when they receive such an assignment they ought to pray to Heavenly Father to learn the topic he would have them speak about. Scott was old enough to do that, and he did. He prayed in his room for a few minutes, then came out and said, 'I can't think of a thing.'"

Scott's parents responded, "Well, go try again, Scott. Ask the Lord to help you know what subject would really help the other children in your Primary. We promise you that he'll tell you."

After a little bit he came back and said, "I think I know what I want to do. I want to talk to them about the story of David and Goliath." And then he added, "I remember something that happened in answer to one of my prayers this very last week, and so I'm also going to talk to them about praying and being close to the Lord."

Not many days later this little boy went into Primary and gave his talk. He was very much touched by the Spirit as he read a few verses from 1 Samuel, chapter 17, about David and Goliath. After Goliath had challenged David and told him, in essence, that he was going to feed him to the buzzards, David gave this great answer:

This day will the Lord deliver thee into mine hand;
and I will smite thee, and take thine head from thee; and I
will give the carcases of the host of the Philistines this day
unto the fowls of the air, and to the wild beasts of the
earth; that all the earth may know that there is a God in
Israel.

And all this assembly shall know that the Lord saveth
not with sword and spear: for the battle is the Lord's, and
he will give you into our hands. (1 Sam. 17:46–47.)

Scott followed that story with a short experience of his own
about how he had been praying for help with a test he had been
studying for and had received an "A" on it. He then bore testimony that the Lord would help even a little boy like him to
have his prayers answered.

The next morning one of the women in the ward called
Scott's mother on the telephone. "I was in Primary yesterday,"
she said, "and I want to know what's happening in your family."

"What do you mean?" the mother asked.

The sister answered, "How is it that your young son can
bear testimony with such fervor and Spirit that it reaches everybody in the whole meeting?"

Scott's mother wasn't sure how to respond. But then the sister continued. "You could tell that he really had a testimony of
the scriptures by the way he read those verses," she said. "He
read those passages with the Spirit of the Lord. When I saw the
sweet feeling and testimony your son had of the scriptures, a
deep desire settled over me. I thought, That's what I want for
my children. I talked it over with my husband—and we want
you to know that we had our first family scripture reading this
morning. We just want to thank you for having such a good
boy."

What a wonderful testimony of the blessings of family
scripture reading. That's where our children also (along with

thousands of other children in the Church) have learned to love the scriptures.

What Is a Family?

As we talk about family scripture study, I would first like to define what I mean by *family*. The obvious answer is a dad and a mom and children together, all reading aloud and discussing the scriptures. But what about a single mom or dad with one or more children? Yes, they should have family scripture study too. What about a newly married couple, or maybe an older couple whose children have gone? Yes, they too would be blessed if they were to study the scriptures together regularly. I would even expand the definition to say that roommates would receive great blessings from studying together, and certainly missionaries are counseled to study the gospel together every day.

I hope, then, that just because you are not part of a traditional family you don't feel this section of the book has no application to you. I believe it does, and I hope it is helpful to people in all circumstances.

I bear my testimony that studying with someone else has a great multiplying effect on our learning. We can learn more truth, and learn it faster, when we study with someone else.

But the key to our greatest growth is to study with someone else *and* at the same time to study on our own. If we will do this, we will be blessed with greater progress, greater understanding, and a greater closeness to the Lord.

As we proceed with this section, you'll see that I use a few examples from my own family, both good and bad. I hesitate to do that, because it is so personal. Unfortunately, however, I have no examples from *your* family to use! (I will change the names of my children to protect their privacy.)

GUIDANCE AND DIRECTION FROM THE SCRIPTURES

Nephi's Testimony

The scriptures themselves are our best source of information and testimony on why families should read scriptures together. One of my favorite scriptures on the scriptures is in 2 Nephi 32, which we discussed in Part 1. Let's review it briefly here in the context of family.

Nephi wrote, "The words of Christ will tell you all things what ye should do." (2 Ne. 32:3.) The scriptures, the living prophets, and personal revelation—all sources of the words of Christ—combine to guide us in all our decisions. They combine to help us know the Lord's will in everything we need to do.

That doesn't necessarily mean that every specific answer to every question is found in the pages of the four standard works. But the principles that govern the answers to those questions are. The scriptures will also guide us to those other vital sources of direction: our living prophets and revelation.

It is important to note that in the same chapter in which Nephi taught us about the words of Christ, he also said, "If ye would hearken unto the Spirit which teacheth a man to pray ye would know that ye must pray; . . . I say unto you that ye must pray always, and not faint; that ye must not perform any thing unto the Lord save in the first place ye shall pray unto the Father in the name of Christ." (2 Ne. 32:8–9.) Why is prayer so important in this context? Because it will help us receive the Holy Ghost, who, in turn, will help us receive revelation (or the words of Christ) to guide us in every part of our lives.

These truths are a great blessing for individuals—but think how blessed a family would be if each member received this kind of help! Family scripture reading will lead family members to great gospel truths that will guide them in their lives—both directly in the pages of the books and also indirectly, by teaching them about the process of prayer and revelation and by motivating them to follow the living prophets.

As they live this kind of life—one in which they are continually seeking and receiving guidance—family members will discover a most valuable additional blessing: In the very process they will be drawing closer to the Lord, strengthening

"WE FEEL THE LOVE"

One Family's Experience

"Regular family scripture study has brought us some real blessings. We have experienced in a small way the promise given in 1 Nephi 15:24: 'Whoso would hearken unto the word of God, and would hold fast unto it, they would never perish; neither could the temptations and the fiery darts of the adversary overpower them.' It has indeed been a little easier for our children to withstand the temptations at school. Scripture reading has also helped us answer the questions of our nonmember neighbors and of acquaintances at school. We feel the love that our Savior and our Heavenly Father have for us as we read their words. We are closer as a family. We want to serve our fellowmen more. We are coming to know our Savior as Alma taught in Alma 32:43: 'Then, my brethren, ye shall reap the rewards of your faith, and your diligence, and patience, and long-suffering, waiting for the tree to bring forth fruit unto you.'

"We still have a long way to go, but finally we have a testimony of reading the scriptures as a family."

their relationship with him, and finding themselves gradually
but surely becoming more like him.

BECOMING "WISE UNTO SALVATION"

Paul's Testimony

In a letter to Timothy, Paul wrote this powerful explanation
of why we need the scriptures:

> But continue thou in the things which thou hast
> learned and hast been assured of, knowing of whom thou
> hast learned them;
> And that from a child thou hast known the holy scrip-
> tures, which are able to make thee wise unto salvation
> through faith which is in Christ Jesus.
> All scripture is given by inspiration of God, and is
> profitable for doctrine, for reproof, for correction, for
> instruction in righteousness:
> That the man of God may be perfect, throughly fur-
> nished unto all good works. (2 Tim. 3:14–17.)

What do the scriptures do for us? They can make us "wise
unto salvation," if we have faith in Jesus Christ. They give us
the things God wants us to know, teaching true doctrine,
reproving us for our sins, and correcting us in our errors. They
teach us the ways of righteousness. If we receive the scriptures,
if we have faith in Christ, if we become men and women of
God, the scriptures can help us become "perfect," giving us all
we need in order to perform "all good works."

In addition, the scriptures can bless us from the time of
childhood, as they did Timothy. Our children, as they learn to
talk and then to read, are not too young to receive great benefits
from the scriptures. *They* can become "wise unto salvation." *They*
can learn the doctrines of the gospel. *They* can be reproved, cor-
rected, and instructed in righteousness. *They* can receive all they

need to be able to do the good works the Lord requires of them. And *they* can advance more surely along the path to perfection.

COMING TO A CHANGE OF HEART

Samuel's Testimony

Samuel the Lamanite gives us another testimony of the value of the scriptures:

> And behold, ye do know of yourselves, for ye have witnessed it, that as many of them as are brought to the knowledge of the truth, and to know of the wicked and abominable traditions of their fathers, and are led to believe the holy scriptures, yea, the prophecies of the holy prophets, which are written, which leadeth them to faith on the Lord, and unto repentance, which faith and repentance bringeth a change of heart unto them—
>
> Therefore, as many as have come to this, ye know of yourselves are firm and steadfast in the faith, and in the thing wherewith they have been made free. (Hel. 15:7–8.)

What wonderful promises for families! Samuel teaches us that believing in the scriptures will help us turn from false traditions. And he teaches that if we receive the scriptures, and come to believe in them, they will lead us to faith, which will lead us to repentance. Faith coupled with repentance will bring us to a change of heart. And those who receive a change of heart "are firm and steadfast in the faith."

These are blessings every righteous parent desires for his or her child: That the child will turn with an honest heart to Christ and receive the blessings of the Atonement, that the child will be "firm and steadfast in the faith" forever.

Are these blessings that families can grow in together as they read the scriptures? It is my testimony that they most assuredly are.

USE SCRIPTURES TO
"BRING OUR CHILDREN TO CHRIST"

Testimonies of Modern Prophets

President Ezra Taft Benson spoke out frequently and clearly on family scripture reading. On one occasion he said: "We have not been using the Book of Mormon as we should. Our homes are not as strong unless we are using it to bring our children to Christ. Our families may be corrupted by worldly trends and teachings unless we know how to use the book to expose and combat the falsehoods in [the world]." (Ezra Taft Benson, *A Witness and a Warning* [Salt Lake City: Deseret Book Co., 1988], 6.)

I bear testimony that if we will raise our family on the scriptures—specifically the Book of Mormon—we will bring our children to Christ. We will find the standard—the Christlike standard—we can use to help our children measure the way they dress, the music they listen to, the things they read, the movies they see. (See Ezra Taft Benson, *Ensign,* May 1986, 78.) The very values of the Lord are found in the scriptures. If our families will read the scriptures prayerfully, those values will begin to be found in our hearts and our homes.

"Let us not treat lightly the great things we have received from the hand of the Lord," President Benson said. "His word is one of the most valuable gifts He has given us. I urge you to recommit yourselves to a study of the scriptures. Immerse yourselves in them daily so you will have the power of the Spirit to attend you in your calling. Read them in your families and teach your children to love and treasure them." (*Ensign,* May 1986, 82.)

I bear witness that if you and your family will faithfully immerse yourselves in the scriptures, you will indeed love and cherish them. You, as a family, will hold them close to your heart. And you will recognize that they are the instrument by which each of you will be converted to God. All that from becoming more involved in consistent and meaningful family scripture reading.

President Gordon B. Hinckley has given us this promise concerning reading the Book of Mormon: "Brothers and sisters, without reservation I promise you that if you will prayerfully read the Book of Mormon, regardless of how many times you previously have read it, there will come into your hearts an added measure of the Spirit of the Lord. There will come a strengthened resolution to walk in obedience to his commandments, and there will come a stronger testimony of the living reality of the Son of God." (*Ensign,* June 1988, 6.)

What parents would not want these blessings for their children? If we will read the Book of Mormon with our children, we can help them lay claim to these promises: "An added measure of the Spirit of the Lord" in their lives, "a strengthened resolution" to be obedient, and "a stronger testimony" of Jesus Christ, our Savior.

Gospel Outcomes

There is another important reason why we should be reading scriptures as a family, and it has to do with a concept called "gospel outcomes."

Some years ago the Church did a study in which they interviewed hundreds of young men to try to discover what determined their faithfulness in the gospel. (Even though this study was directed at young men, we have every reason to think it would be equally true of young women.) The first goal of the study was to find out what parents most wanted for their young men in terms of activity in the Church. The researchers learned that there were four "gospel outcomes" that were more important than all others. Parents wanted their sons to receive the Melchizedek Priesthood, to be endowed, to go on missions, and to be sealed in the temple.

The next step of the study looked at the young men. They were placed into two categories. One category was boys who received the Melchizedek Priesthood, went on missions, and went to the temple; the other category was boys who did none of those things. The objective was to try to find out what made the difference between the two groups. Why did the boys in one category have the gospel outcomes their parents had hoped for, while the boys in the other category did not? What was the role of seminary, peers, Aaronic Priesthood quorum advisers, and family? What made a real difference in the lives of these young men?

The answer that came back was so strikingly simple that many struggled to comprehend it. The researchers learned that two basic practices had a far greater impact on gospel outcomes than any of the others: (1) Personal prayer and (2) personal scripture study, both listed under the heading "Personal Worship of God."

GOSPEL OUTCOMES	Ordination to Melchizedek Priesthood	Receive Temple Endowment	Serve a Full-Time Mission	Marry in the Temple

↑

PERSONAL WORSHIP	1. Personal prayer 2. Personal scripture study

In their conclusion, the researchers said, in essence, you show me a boy who's having a personal prayer every day, and who combines that with daily scripture study, and I will show you a boy who goes on a mission and to the temple.

Could it be that simple, that young boys and girls who pray and read the scriptures will have the gospel outcomes we all desire? I believe in large measure that that is so.

The next question the researchers asked was this: If personal prayer and personal scripture study lead to the gospel outcomes we desire, how do you get young men and women to pray and study?

They came back with three answers, which they categorized under "Family Worship of God."

1. Have family prayer. Show us a family that's having family prayer, they said, and we'll show you a boy who's learning how to have his personal prayers.

2. Have family scripture study and family home evening. Show us a family that's regularly reading the scriptures together, they said, and we'll show you a boy who's reading the scriptures on his own.

3. Teach and exemplify the Lord's values. Somehow the values of the Lord have to transfer from one generation, the adults, to the young people. The families that learn to do this are those that have the best gospel outcomes.

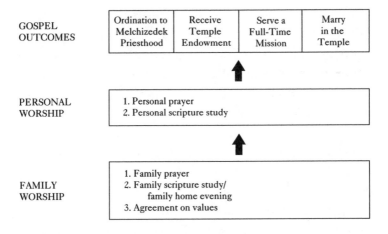

GOSPEL OUTCOMES	Ordination to Melchizedek Priesthood	Receive Temple Endowment	Serve a Full-Time Mission	Marry in the Temple

PERSONAL WORSHIP	1. Personal prayer 2. Personal scripture study

FAMILY WORSHIP	1. Family prayer 2. Family scripture study/ family home evening 3. Agreement on values

Before we leave the study on gospel outcomes, there is one more question we need to look at. The researchers asked, "What is the impact of the Church on these outcomes?" The answer was both surprising and enlightening. They learned that the Church helps and supports parents in their teaching. But the real battle is won in the home—the home is what asserts the greatest influence on our youth.

How important is family scripture reading? How important is family prayer? How important is the teaching and example of parents? These are all-important! If we are consistent in these things, our children will be much more likely to read scriptures and to pray on their own—and when they do that they will be much more likely to receive their temple endowments, go on missions, and be married in the temple.

A PROPHET'S EMPHASIS

We can marshal many excellent arguments to show why we should read scriptures together as a family—but perhaps the most compelling argument for me is that our living prophets have encouraged us to do so.

I know without a doubt that prophets speak by inspiration of the Lord and that they guide us, as directed by the Lord, in the things we should do. Let me give you a couple of examples of how the presidents of the Church have known what to emphasize, even though the future they saw so clearly might have been obscure to everyone else.

When Heber J. Grant was president of the Church, he was noted for teaching one theme over and over again. He tirelessly emphasized the Word of Wisdom, feeling impressed to do so because we had a generation of Church members who were not very obedient to that commandment. He also knew something else—that prophets teach not only their present generation but the one that's coming up.

Once a man sent a letter to President Grant saying, "President, we really appreciate all these talks on the Word of Wisdom, but don't you have some other talk?" President Grant turned to his secretary and said, "Well, it looks like someone still hasn't got it." And at the next conference he spoke on the Word of Wisdom once again.

What happened to the next generation? Everything broke loose—alcohol, tobacco, and drugs were more commonly used than ever. What would have happened to that generation of the Church's youth if President Grant had not known what to emphasize—and if the generation of his time had not been obedient to his counsel?

What did President David O. McKay teach so strongly over and over and over again?

"No other success can compensate for failure in the home." He spoke out strongly about marriage, about nurturing the love between husband and wife, about the evils of divorce.

And now what are we seeing in our generation? Single-parent families are becoming more and more the norm. Divorce has been called an epidemic. Those who did not listen to the prophet have suffered the terrible consequences.

And now we come to our own generation. The presidents in the last couple of decades have emphasized a number of things—repentance, missionary work, temple attendance, and so forth—but one thing that stands out, because of its frequency, is the continuing emphasis on strengthening families. And what is one of the best ways to accomplish that? It is through reading the scriptures as individuals, as families, and as a Church. Why is our study of scripture so important? Because it will give us a foundation in understanding and testimony that will enable us to stand firm, both individually and as families, against the winds of trials to come.

If we will build our foundation on the word of God, we will be able to stand faithfully through the many trials that are yet to be poured out upon all the earth. But if we neglect the counsel of our prophets, both we and our families may suffer.

This is a powerful convincing factor for me as a father. I want to be sure that we seek to read the scriptures every single day, to see that my children's testimonies are rooted in the holy word of the Lord, helping to make their testimonies unshakable.

A PROMISE FROM THE LORD

Some years ago when I was organizing a stake I interviewed an acquaintance of mine who, if I remember correctly, was serving as a stake clerk at the time. He was a faithful man in every respect. He went to all of his meetings, paid his tithing, was praying regularly, and was diligent in keeping the commandments. His wife and most of his children were as faithful as he was.

He told me in the process of the interview, however, that he had not been reading the scriptures with his family as he should. I felt impressed to bear to him my testimony of the power of family scripture reading. In that moment, when the Spirit was strong, he confided in me that his youngest son, who was sixteen years old, had begun to stray from the Church. He was doing very poorly in school and on several occasions had threatened to leave home. The father felt helpless to make a difference in his son's life.

Again I felt impressed to tell him that if he would begin to faithfully study the scriptures with his family, the Lord would deliver his son from the bondage he was entering into. I couldn't promise that it would happen immediately—but I knew that, in time, the Lord would answer his pleas for his son.

He seemed to be touched by that promise. What I didn't know then, but learned later, was that he went into the outer office and sobbed for joy. "I felt within my heart that the Lord had spoken directly to me through you," he said later. "I knew he had given me a promise he would not break, if I would but do my part."

Later in the day when I met his wife (whom I also knew), I

reaffirmed to her what I'd felt to say to her husband. She committed, as he had done, that they would begin to have family scripture study.

Because of the number of people one meets in stake conferences from week to week, I had forgotten about that promise. Some two years went by. One evening I was downtown with my wife and other family members when this good brother approached me.

He said, "I want to give you an accounting of what has happened in the last two years. I took the promise you gave to me in the name of the Lord that if I would be faithful in my family scripture study, the Lord would deliver my son. I now have a strong testimony of the power of scripture reading in a family. I am unable to say exactly how it worked. The only thing I know is that we have been reading together faithfully for the last couple of years, and my son has totally turned around. He repented of his sins and fasted and prayed and received a patriarchal blessing. He has a 4.0 grade point average at the university. This Sunday he will be ordained an elder. He's nearly prepared for his mission and is on his way to being a faithful elder in Israel. How thankful I am that that promise was given and that the Lord fulfilled it as you promised he would."

I was humbled to hear his testimony of their experience and told him I would be honored to meet his son. At the time of this writing, this wonderful young man is serving a mission.

I bear testimony that the power of family scripture reading will indeed bring our children to Christ, if we will do it in a loving, kind, patient, and consistent way.

The Blessings of Family Scripture Study

So why is it that we should be reading the scriptures with our families? Here is a summary of the reasons we have discussed in this and other chapters, plus a few other reasons for good measure:

• Family scripture reading helps us hold onto our children—or helps us regain them if they have begun to stray, as the story just related demonstrates.

• We have been counseled by our prophets to read together—and we should be obedient to their counsel.

• The scriptures can help each family member know more about Christ and develop a testimony of his atonement, his love, and his power to bless us.

• The scriptures can help each family member find answers to the problems in their lives. They help us receive direction from the Lord.

"We Are Grateful"— A Success Story

One Family's Experience

"Our family began a regular habit of family scripture reading and study several years ago. We tried a few different approaches; finally we settled on having each person read the Book of Mormon, a column in turn. Where appropriate, we would stop the reading and make comments, ask questions, and take advantage of teaching moments. Each time we completed the Book of Mormon, we started at First Nephi, chapter one, again the next week.

"The blessings we have

• They help us draw closer together as a family, just because we're doing something important together. Reading scriptures together will help unify a family, cause them to pull together more, and help them be one as Latter-day Saints.

• They help a family draw closer to the Holy Spirit because he's present testifying of the truthfulness of what we're reading.

• They help children learn how to study. I have been amazed to hear my own children say, as they have gotten a little older, "I first learned to read in the Book of Mormon." What a blessing parents can convey to their children!

received from being obedient to this counsel are more important than the mechanics of how it gets done. We know that once we became regular at this practice, peace prevailed in our home as never before. Much of the contention essentially vanished. Our youngest child even wrote a paper for school on how well our family members got along with each other.

"This youngest child was in first grade when we began our reading together. She was in a remedial reading class, reading below her grade level, and needing extra help. She sat on my lap as I pointed out the words as they were read. After a while, she started reading one verse at a time. She fairly quickly became quite good at reading, and by the time she entered second grade she was reading on the third-grade level. I attribute this success to reading the Book of Mormon.

"Our children, as well as my husband and I, have gained a deep knowledge and testimony of this great work of the ancient prophets, which Heavenly Father has preserved for us. We are grateful for the Book of Mormon and for the wisdom of our Church leaders to counsel us to read and study it as a family. We know it is true and that it truly blesses our lives."

• Reading scriptures together helps us learn how to read and speak Heavenly Father's language. Even children can begin to learn that language—both the unusual words of the scriptures and the language of the Spirit.

• The experience of reading together engenders humility and increases love in the family. It builds our faith.

• Reading together helps our children learn to see the Lord's servants as heroes. They want to be like Nephi going after the brass plates. They want to go forth as Ammon did, boldly venturing among the Lamanites without fear and bearing his testimony. What great heroes we find in the scriptures—and what a blessing to a family if parents will teach their children about those heroes.

• Reading together helps a family worship together. Through that process, it helps to bring a daily focus on God and on the needs of other people—and thus it brings about repentance and a desire to change.

• Reading together creates a wonderful opportunity for sharing, for understanding one another, for listening, for seeing the Lord speak in revelation to the hearts of each family member.

• Family scripture reading creates a perfect opportunity for parents to bear testimony to their children, and for children to bear testimony to each other. That process of sharing testimony can truly strengthen children in their conversion to the Lord. As Paul said, "Faith cometh by hearing, and hearing by the word of God." (Rom. 10:17.)

CHAPTER 13

PRIME TIME FOR
TEACHING AND TESTIMONY

Some years ago one of our daughters was being tempted—and pressured—by some friends to dress in inappropriate ways. It was not nearly as serious as it could have been (it mostly concerned styles of jewelry), but the styles she was being attracted to were rather worldly. Her mother and I had talked to her more than once, but we could tell we hadn't yet reached her heart. She knew what was right, but she hadn't come to a final decision about what she was going to do.

One morning, right when things were reaching a crisis point, we came to 2 Nephi 13 in our family scripture reading. In verse 16 we read: "Moreover, the Lord saith: Because the daughters of Zion are haughty, and walk with stretched-forth necks and wanton eyes, walking and mincing as they go . . ." Does that sound like a worldly woman? Then we came to verse 19, where it says the women were wearing "the chains and the bracelets, and the . . . bonnets, and the ornaments of the legs, and the headbands, . . . and the ear-rings; the rings, and nose jewels; . . . and the crisping-pins; [and] the glasses [which means transparent clothing]." (See 2 Ne. 13:16, 19–23.)

After we read those verses, I bore testimony to the whole family about the importance of being modest, of not calling too much attention to yourself by the way you dress and by the jewelry you wear. I wasn't directing my words right to this

149

daughter because I didn't want to embarrass her, but I hoped with all my being she was listening.

At the very moment of my testimony, I saw, as it were, the words penetrate my daughter's heart. I saw the Lord say to her through the words in that scripture and through the testimony I offered, "This is correct and right, and you will be greatly blessed if you obey." And in response I saw her say in her heart, "I will do it." I saw her heart change in just those few minutes.

The issue was never brought up with this daughter again— nor did it need to be. That morning in scripture reading the Lord sent the blessing we sought—a blessing that came by the power of love, of testimony, of the scriptures, and of his words. There are few times when parents have a better opportunity to teach and to testify than during family scripture time. In fact, that is one of the major blessings of family scripture study—it gives parents a golden opportunity, day after day, to instill in their children the truths that are most important to them.

TEACHING THE LORD'S VALUES

In the previous chapter we talked about "gospel outcomes." What most influences young men and young women to go on missions, receive their temple endowments, and be sealed to an eternal partner in the temple? The answer had three parts: personal prayer (which is often motivated by family prayer), personal scripture reading (which is often motivated by family scripture reading), and personally holding the Lord's values (which often stems from parental teaching of those values).

Let me give you an example of the importance of teaching the Lord's values in the home—and how the scriptures can help in that effort. Many parents have had the experience where a son or daughter comes to them and says, "Why are we the only family in the whole neighborhood who . . . ?"

There are many phrases that might fill in the blank:

" . . . has a midnight curfew?"

" . . . has to go to church every single Sunday?"

" . . . can't wear short shorts?"

" . . . has to do chores?"

(The next phrase is usually: "None of my friends has to . . .")

Suppose one of your children were to come to you and ask, "Why are we the only family in the whole neighborhood that doesn't watch television on Sunday?

You might be inclined to say, "Because I said so. That's just the way it is." Or, "That's just one of our family rules." Or, "Because it's the right thing to do."

But better than any of those responses would be to take an approach where you teach the Lord's values. Suppose you were a dad talking to his daughter. You could take her into her bedroom and sit together, opening the Doctrine and Covenants to section 59.

"Honey, maybe I've never really shared with you how I feel about the Sabbath, and what I've learned from the Lord. Let's look at these verses together:

"'And that thou mayest more fully keep thyself unspotted from the world, thou shalt go to the house of prayer and offer up thy sacraments upon my holy day; For verily this is a day appointed unto you'—listen to this, honey, and see what two things the Lord has given us to do on his day—'to rest from your labors, and to pay thy devotions unto the Most High.' I think that's saying we should go to church and find ways to do the Lord's work—it's saying we ought to serve, pray, help others, and learn ourselves. ' . . . Remember that on this, the Lord's day, thou shalt offer thine oblations and thy sacraments unto the Most High. . . . And on this day thou shalt do none other thing.'" (D&C 59:9–10, 12–13.)

After having shared the Lord's words in the scriptures, you might bear a fervent testimony to your daughter. "Honey, I want you to know that I know, with all my heart, that this is the word of the Lord. This is how the Lord wants us to observe his Sabbaths, and that's why your mom and I decided that watching television on Sunday just isn't a very good thing to do."

If you were to do that in great love, your child might say, "Well, you know, Dad, I guess I never understood it quite that way. I didn't realize the Lord said that so strongly. I do believe what you're saying, and I think that is the best choice for me and for our family."

By that kind of process, a value might be transferred by the Spirit from one generation to another, from a father or mother to a daughter or son. Values transfer in other ways as well—through family prayer, family scripture reading, family home evening, informal teaching and testifying moments, and, of course, example.

IDEAS FOR BETTER TEACHING

Mom and Dad Get Up First

To be able to do their best as teachers, I think it is crucial for Dad and Mom to get up first in the morning (if you're reading in the morning). Think of how they can bless their family if they will make sure they have the Spirit of the Lord with them before they call the children together for scripture reading. If Dad and Mom drag in at the same time as the children, barely more awake than the children and poorly prepared, they'll have a harder time bringing the Lord's Spirit into the meeting. But if they get up just a little earlier, prepare, awaken fully, and obtain the Spirit, they'll be much better teachers when the family assembles.

Prepare Your Heart

Whenever you begin to read the scriptures, it's essential that you be prepared in your heart. In Part 1 of this book we discussed how the scriptures are like a Liahona—they will speak to you through the Spirit of the Lord if you're open while you're reading. The two most important things you can do to prepare yourself for such a blessing are to pray and humble yourself. Families can receive the same blessing on the same basis.

The scriptures teach us that if you do not pray, you will not understand what you're reading. (Read D&C 32:4, below, in reverse—what happens if you do not pray?) But if you do pray for understanding, the Lord will unfold the meaning of the scriptures to you. Here is the Lord's promise:

> And they shall give heed to that which is written, and pretend to no other revelation; and they shall pray always that I may unfold the same to their understanding. (D&C 32:4.)

It is also crucial that we be humble. If we're not humble and teachable, we will block the Spirit and thus will find it difficult to learn from Him while we're reading the scriptures. As the Lord said in the Doctrine and Covenants,

> Let him that is ignorant learn wisdom by humbling himself and calling upon the Lord his God, that his eyes may be opened that he may see, and his ears opened that he may hear;
> For my Spirit is sent forth into the world to enlighten the humble and contrite, and to the condemnation of the ungodly. (D&C 136:32–33.)

Parents should teach family members to come to scripture reading time in a spirit of prayer and humility. If you do, you will truly feel the Spirit of the Lord.

Fill in the White Spaces

One valuable thing parents can do is help their children learn to "fill in the white spaces" on the page. As you look at a book of scripture, you'll see the black print, which gives us the words of the Lord. Those words are the important message the Lord is giving to all of us. But you will also notice that there are a lot of white spaces. If you're prayerfully reading scriptures, the Lord will speak to you in your heart, giving you revelation to help you know how to apply those verses to yourself—in essence, he will fill in the white spaces for you.

Parents can try to teach family members how to hear the promptings of the Spirit, how to hear the voice of the Lord when they're reading the scriptures with the family. Then, when they're reading alone, they will know how to follow that same process on their own.

Group Involvement

I once heard that there are three rules for good teaching (I know this is oversimplifying), and these certainly apply in family scripture reading time: Involve them, involve them, involve them.

Sometimes dads and moms have a tendency to just talk, talk, talk, or to preach, preach, preach. That doesn't usually make for a very good scripture reading experience. Children need to be involved. They need to help with the teaching. They need to be asking questions. The more you can involve them, the better the experience will be. (I'll talk more about how to do that in the next chapter.)

Ask Questions

Please remember this important teaching principle: It is better to ask than to tell. *Ask* your children about what you're reading to the family. Don't tell them all the answers. Get them to think about the meaning of what you're reading and to tell you what they think. More important, get them to tell you what they feel.

Mom and Dad, be careful not to set yourselves up as a light

to your children. Let the Lord be the light, and let the Lord's Spirit be the teacher.

In the best family scripture reading experience, Mom and Dad and the children together will be seeking instruction from the Lord. Let your children ask questions of you, and then let each person ask questions, in his or her heart, of the Spirit. If parents will do that, they will be much better teachers in scripture reading.

Be Patient

Remember to be patient with your little children. Many times they genuinely don't understand, even though we may think they do.

Once not long ago I was worried about a big snowstorm that was coming—it was predicted that a full foot would fall in our area. Our yard was unprepared for winter, and I was anxious to get home from work to prepare for the snow.

When I arrived, obviously in a hurry, my eight-year-old son said, "Hey, Dad, don't worry about the snow. It's not going to bother us."

"Why not?" I said. "The weatherman said we'll have a foot of snow by morning."

He said, "No, I just heard the weather, and he said it was only going to snow on the benches." In Utah, the benches are the areas right next to the mountains, which is where we lived at the time. My son thought it was going to snow on the benches where people sit, but not on our yard.

Again, be patient with little children because sometimes they genuinely don't understand. We need to move along at a pace they can handle.

Don't Give Up

Finally, don't give up. Work out the contention that is continually sown by Satan—he will try to get family members upset at one another so you won't have the Spirit in scripture reading.

Don't give up. It's worth it to persist. And if you will, I promise you in the name of the Lord that He will sow peace and harmony in our families.

Here is a wonderful promise we find in the Book of Mormon: The writings of the scriptures shall come forth "unto the confounding of false doctrines and laying down of contentions, and establishing peace." (2 Ne. 3:12.)

TESTIMONY FROM A PROPHET

In our teaching, we would do well to consistently testify of the truth of that which we've taught. When I was a missionary serving in South America, I had an experience that taught me as never before the great blessing of hearing a fervent testimony. I already had a testimony of the Book of Mormon. In fact, when I was twelve years old, I had read the Book of Mormon on my own and knew without any question that the Book of Mormon was the word of God. I didn't understand all the words, but I knew that the book was of the Lord.

In those days General Authorities interviewed all the missionaries when they came on their periodic tours. It was our privilege to have President Joseph Fielding Smith (then president of the Council of the Twelve) in our mission conducting meetings, giving direction to the president, and interviewing missionaries.

When it was my turn to be interviewed, he had been meeting with missionaries for many hours. I knew he was tired—after all, he was in his eighties and had talked to many missionaries that day. I thought to myself, "I'd like to ask him a question, but I won't because I'm sure he must be exhausted."

I went into the room. He had me sit across from him, with a little, rickety table between us. He put his hands on the table and said, "Elder Cook, are you faithful?"

"Yes."

"Are you keeping the commandments?"

"I am."

"Are you obeying all the mission rules?" He continued with those kinds of questions; then, when he was finished, he said, "Well, I commend you for that, Elder. Go ahead faithfully and be a wonderful missionary. We love you for keeping your life in order."

I shook hands with this wonderful man, a prophet of the Lord, told him I loved him, and got up and walked to the door. As I took hold of the door handle to leave, he said, "Elder Cook, wait a minute. You have a question, don't you?"

I turned back and said, "Well, I did have, but I know you've been here a long time, President, and it's fine. I'll work it through."

"No," he said. "You come back." He had me sit back down. "Now what's your question, Elder?"

"Well, this may sound like a silly question to you, President Smith, but I'll ask anyway. I've always known the Book of Mormon is true—I have no doubt that it is the word of God. But am I supposed to have an independent testimony that Joseph Smith was a prophet? Or is it sufficient just to believe he was because I know he couldn't have translated the Book of Mormon unless he was? Am I supposed to have a separate testimony, independent of the Book of Mormon, about Joseph Smith himself?"

This great man then did something for me that I will never forget. I've since done it with my children. In fact, I've done it in every circumstance where I've wanted to have the help of the Spirit in convincing someone else of a truth. President Smith simply said, "Elder Cook, in the year 1820 there was a young man by the name of Joseph Smith. He was confused about religion." He then recounted to me the Joseph Smith story. By that time in my life, I'm sure I had read that story many times—and he surely knew I was very familiar with it—but he recounted it to me in great detail. Near the end of the story he said, "Joseph Smith saw a light descend from heaven, brighter than the sun at noonday. It descended until it rested upon him. And in that light he saw two personages. One of them called him by name, saying 'Joseph, This is my beloved Son. Hear him.'" When he was finished, he said, "I bear witness to you, Elder Cook, in the name of Jesus Christ, that Joseph Smith is a prophet of God."

Tears were in his eyes—and in mine as well. I felt the Spirit of the Lord fill me full, as if I had been an empty tank. When I walked out of that room, I had an independent testimony of my own that Joseph Smith was a prophet of God. It has been with me ever since. I have since marveled how one person with the Spirit of the Lord could so touch another to bring about such a great blessing.

BRINGING TESTIMONY INTO THE HOME

As the father of eight children, I have seen the power of testimony again and again as we have talked about observance of the Sabbath, tithing, chastity, prayer, or any of the other doctrines of the Church. A sincere, earnest testimony from Dad and Mom, borne with the Spirit of the Lord, can have the same impact on your children as President Smith's testimony had on me as a young missionary. Faith comes "by hearing the word of the Lord," as we quoted from Paul earlier. I bear witness that that is a true principle. And it again underscores how important it is that we have the Spirit with us in great abundance while we're having our scripture reading as families.

Incidentally, Joseph Smith's story gives us another reason for family scripture study. As I have thought of his experience, I've wondered, Why was Joseph Smith reading in the Bible anyway? What motivated him to be reading in James?

Some years later he recorded in his journal:

Notwithstanding the corruptions and abominations of the times, and the evil spirit manifested towards us on account of our belief in the Book of Mormon, at many places and among various persons, yet the Lord continued His watchful care and loving kindness to us day by day; and we made it a rule wherever there was an opportunity, to read a chapter in the Bible, and pray; and these seasons of worship gave us great consolation. (*History of the Church of Jesus Christ of Latter-day Saints,* ed. B. H. Roberts, 7 vols. [Salt Lake City: The Church of Jesus Christ of Latter-day Saints, 1902–1932], 1:188.)

Where do you think he learned the blessings of scripture reading? From his father and mother in his home, in family scripture study. What an impact that teaching had on this young prophet! Because of his home training, he was prepared to go to the Bible when he had a problem, and he was able to find that impressive statement from James: "If any of you lack wisdom, let him ask of God." (James 1:5.)

We can bless our children as Joseph's parents blessed him. Of course our children may not become the founding prophets of a dispensation, but they can all become "prophets" in the sense that they will know the voice of the Spirit, seek it, and follow it. The foundation for so many of the spiritual blessings we desire for our children is family prayer, family home evening, and family scripture reading.

A PERSONAL BLESSING

Several years ago one of our sons was sick. I'll call him John to protect his privacy. His mom and I had subtly encouraged him to seek a priesthood blessing.

Despite our gentle suggestions, he didn't ever ask. His sickness lasted one day, two days, and still he didn't seek a blessing. One morning we were reading scriptures as a family, and we read a statement about good health in Alma. We then read the cross-reference in Doctrine and Covenants 42:

> And whosoever among you are sick, and have not faith to be healed, but believe, shall be nourished with all tenderness, with herbs and mild food, and that not by the hand of an enemy.
>
> And the elders of the church, two or more, shall be called, and shall pray for and lay their hands upon them in my name; and if they die they shall die unto me, and if they live they shall live unto me. . . .
>
> And again, it shall come to pass that he that hath faith in me to be healed, and is not appointed unto death, shall be healed. (D&C 42:43–44, 48.)

We next read in the book of James, where he asks, "Is any sick among you?" Does the next phrase say "call the doctor"? No, it says, "let him call for the elders of the church." (Of course, that doesn't mean we can't utilize doctors, but we do need to start with a focus on the Lord.) Here's the whole passage:

> Is any sick among you? let him call for the elders of the church; and let them pray over him, anointing him with oil in the name of the Lord:
>
> And the prayer of faith shall save the sick, and the Lord shall raise him up; and if he have committed sins, they shall be forgiven him.
>
> . . . pray one for another, that ye may be healed. The effectual fervent prayer of a righteous man availeth much. (James 5:14–16.)

After reading those scriptures, we bore testimony to our family of the power of priesthood blessings, if we exercise faith.

Scripture reading ended. We said no more. About five minutes later John came to me in a very humble spirit. He said, rather emotionally, "Dad, would you feel okay about giving me a priesthood blessing?"

"Would you like me to, John?"

"Yes, I would. I really believe the Lord could heal me. I believe what we read this morning."

In those few moments, as we read those scriptures and shared testimony together, I saw a change of heart in that boy. I did administer to him, and by afternoon he was feeling much better. The next morning he was off to school, counting his blessings that the Lord had answered a young man's prayer. And we were counting our blessings that we had the practice of reading scriptures in our family, and that the Lord had blessed us with his Spirit.

AVOIDING PITFALLS
AND ROADBLOCKS

"I'm sure our family fits right in with many other families in the Church," writes one busy, typical family. "We wanted to try to find the time to have family scripture study, but there just didn't seem to be enough hours in the day. One Sunday our bishop was inspired to tell us that we needed to get our priorities in order (something we knew but needed to hear again). If we weren't having family prayer, scripture study, family home evening, and so forth, we needed to remove whatever obstacles were keeping us from them.

"At the time, our daughter was spending twenty hours a week in gymnastics, which, combined with school, left little else in her life. Not only did her gymnastics cost more money than we had, but it left us no time to read scriptures together. We felt it was an answer to prayer when she finally decided to try something else. Too bad that it wasn't that simple. Whenever we would get rid of one thing another seemed to take its place. The adversary didn't want us to have the blessings that reading the scriptures would bring.

"The time of early morning seminary also posed an obstacle. Five o'clock in the morning seemed a bit too early for scripture study. We did have family prayer then, but we could barely keep our eyes open for that. Larry's work would sometimes take him away even before that time. Both kids had paper routes that needed to be done right after school. Jazz Choir took our son away from home as many as two to three afternoons per week. We have two children—I can't imagine keeping up with ten.

"When we did have scripture study, my son seemed bored. He already knew what we were reading. On the other hand, my daughter didn't have the foggiest idea what we were talking about. Trying to keep the Spirit was a real challenge. Nothing seemed to go right. Whenever we seemed to be going in the right direction we ended up taking a few steps backwards."

Does any of this sound familiar? Sometimes the obstacles to reading scriptures as a family seem nothing less than insurmountable. But if we will persist, the rewards will come. This family concludes their account by saying, "After many trials and errors, we finally found a time that works for us all. It has taken a lot of sacrifice on the part of each of us. We are far from perfect and still miss on occasion. But our Heavenly Father is blessing us for making the effort."

Why Do We Struggle to Read?

If reading the scriptures is as important as it appears to be, then why don't we do it? What obstacles stand in our way? What are the pitfalls and roadblocks? Why do we struggle so much with this principle? As I have talked to people about this problem, they've given the following responses (some of which fit closely with the account we just shared):

"We're just not in the habit."

"Our family's schedule makes it too hard. People are going and coming so much that it's very difficult to find a time that works."

"We have other things on our minds. It never seems to be a very high priority."

"We just keep putting it off."

"It takes more energy and effort than we seem to have."

"The scriptures are too boring and too hard for our children to understand."

"We just don't have enough time."

"I guess we just don't have a strong enough testimony of reading scriptures together."

"It seems that Satan doesn't want us to read the scriptures."

"I suspect that one of the reasons we don't read is that we have too much pride."

WHAT GETS IN OUR WAY?

I have given those reasons without comment, but now I would like to take an individual look at each of these obstacles to family scripture reading.

"We're just not in the habit." I suppose it's not ever appropriate to blame our behavior on habit. Habits are made and broken and replaced by new habits according to our true desires. The real reason here is "We don't really want to."

"Our family's schedule makes it too hard. People are going and coming so much that it's very difficult to find a time that works." Perhaps such families need to cut back a little. Or they may need to get up earlier. Or they may need to find a time when *most* of the family members can be present even if all can't.

"We have other things on our minds. It never seems to be a very high priority." Often these are worldly or transitory things. We may be worried about work, school, friends, and so forth. I have found it to be a helpful mindset to be worried first about the Lord and what he would have me do. Then all other things seem to fall into place, even though sometimes it may be hard.

"We just keep putting it off." This goes back to desire. When things are truly important to us, we're able to find a way to get them into place in our lives.

"It takes more energy and effort than we seem to have." Reading the scriptures together does indeed take energy and effort. But I

have learned, as have many others, that you never have a spiritual experience with your family and then regret the effort it took. And spiritual experiences are what come to us when we read scriptures as a family.

"The scriptures are too boring and too hard to understand for our children." This is a common problem in families. But, in general, I feel the problem is really the parents', not the children's. Perhaps Dad and Mom need to learn how to bring the scriptures alive, how to have more fun while they are reading. (I'll give some suggestions on this in following chapters.)

"We just don't have enough time." We all have time for the things that are most important to us. When people tell me they don't have time, I ask them, "In your home yesterday, how long was the television on?" Then they usually admit, "Well, maybe we're just using our time in the wrong way."

I like this statement from Elder Neal A. Maxwell of the Council of the Twelve:

> With true perspective comes a sense of proportion about life. Proportion would help us with our priorities. For instance, clearly one would not forgo partaking of the sacrament because he is trying to lose weight, yet some neglect the scriptures because they are too busy minding the cares of the world. (*Things As They Really Are* [Salt Lake City: Deseret Book Co., 1978], 5.)

"I guess we just don't have a strong enough testimony of reading scriptures together." This may be at the bottom of the whole problem. This fits with a very telling scripture in Mosiah: "And now because of their unbelief they could not understand the word of God; and their hearts were hardened." (Mosiah 26:3.) It also fits with this one from the Doctrine and Covenants: "And your minds in times past have been darkened because of unbelief, and because you have treated lightly the things you have

received—Which vanity and unbelief have brought the whole church under condemnation." (D&C 84:54–55.)

There is a divine purpose behind our having family scripture

"OUR GREATEST CHALLENGE"

One Family's Experience

"Our greatest challenge is not just differing family schedules but *continually changing* family schedules. At times we have resorted to reward systems, such as computer time in trade for participation in family scripture time, but we discovered that the need for this extra motivation was short-lived.

"At first we would not hold scripture study if everyone did not come, but we quickly found this to be a mistake. Now we hold it regardless of who shows up, and most of the time everyone participates. We now have a precise starting time, but we anticipate that this may not always be the case. We know we will always have to adapt to new phases in family life.

"We find that it is still a real challenge to keep it up. It is still not a 'given thing,' but we have had some wonderful discussions about the gospel plan and the values that we hold dear. It definitely gives us a fortifying feeling to begin our day. We also feel that it has helped to curb our ADD (Attention Deficit Disorder) son's anger outbursts, and it gives us all a greater sense of family security and solidarity. As our thirteen-year-old son says, 'It's a lot easier not to do it, but our family seems happier and has less contention when we do.'"

study. If we can become convinced of that spiritually, if we can have testimonies of it, then we'll have enough strength to do it.

"It seems Satan doesn't want us to read the scriptures." He throws up obstacles in our path, and we let him. President Ezra Taft Benson said: "Children, support your parents in their efforts to have daily family scripture study. Pray for them as they pray for you. The adversary does not want scripture study to take place in our homes, and so he will create problems if he can. But we must persist." (*Ensign*, May 1986, 78.)

On one occasion I heard President Benson publicly say, "I don't think I've ever known a time when there was more contention in the Benson household than when we tried to get everybody together for scripture reading."

Those who have tried to read scriptures as a family know that that is all too true—which is a great witness to me that such a practice is extremely important. Otherwise, why would Satan invest that kind of effort in trying to dissuade us from doing it? (But we must also remember the promise of the prophets: if we persist, the contention will melt away and the influence of the Spirit of the Lord will increase.)

"I suspect that one of the reasons we don't read is that we have too much pride." Sometimes parents say, "Well, my children know more than I do. They've been to seminary. If we read scriptures together, I'll be embarrassed because they know twice as much as I do." My answer to that is this: I guess Dad and Mom will just have to humble themselves, admit their weakness, and learn from their children.

THE PROBLEM OF PRIDE

There is another form of pride that keeps us from doing what's right. Surprisingly, some people don't do what the prophet or the Lord asks because they want to choose their own way without others telling them what to do. That kind of pride will keep us from the Lord's kingdom—and, unfortunately, it can hurt our families as well.

I am sobered by these words of the Lord:

> And that wicked one cometh and taketh away light and truth, through disobedience, from the children of men, and because of the tradition of their fathers.
>
> But I have commanded you to bring up your children in light and truth. (D&C 93:39–40.)

I am convinced that one of the prerequisites to our being able to bring up our children in light and truth is for us, as fathers and mothers, to humble ourselves. We need to turn our hearts and our minds over to God, letting him guide us in all we do. If we will humble ourselves and set aside our pride, we will then know that our own wisdom, our own judgments, our own priorities must be placed in a secondary position to those of the Lord.

"My thoughts are not your thoughts, neither are your ways my ways, saith the Lord." (Isa. 55:8.) Those who follow the Lord's ways, letting him establish their path and their pattern in life, are able to find success and blessings for themselves and their families.

To submit in this way is to reject pride and to walk in humility and obedience before the Lord—which is the path that will bring us to his promises.

AGE-OLD EXCUSES

The obstacles that prevent us from reading scriptures as a family are not new. In fact, families have probably been facing these issues (or variations of them) as long as there have been printed scriptures.

Nearly one hundred years ago, Elder Abraham O. Woodruff of the Council of the Twelve gave this motivating testimony of reading scriptures as a family. Note the obstacles he mentions—and the promised blessings:

> We are such a busy lot of people that we do not appear to have time to serve the Lord. . . . At least, we do not take time to serve the Lord. A short time ago I went into the home of Brother Wm. H. Seegmiller, president of the Sevier Stake of Zion, and I was very much impressed with the beautiful practice he has in his home at their devotional exercises. When we got up in the morning we were invited into his parlor, and there one of his daughters played the organ, and we all sang a hymn; then one of the members of the family read a chapter from the Book of Mormon, at the close of which we engaged in prayer. Altogether it took us about twenty minutes or half an hour, and there was a beautiful spirit in that home by reason of this practice.
>
> I thought to myself, what a glorious thing it would be if all the Saints of God would take half an hour every morning to serve Him in this way, and thus assist in setting their own houses in order. . . . The chapter read from the Book of Mormon, or from the Doctrine and Covenants, or from the Bible, would be with us during the day, and our reflections would be upon that which it contained. I believe that the men and women in Israel who take time to do this will succeed in saving their sons and daughters; for such a practice cannot help but have a remarkably good influence upon the children.
>
> But we say we have not time, or we cannot get our families together. Where that is the case, we ought to begin to educate ourselves to carry out this plan, in order to fit and qualify ourselves for something better and greater. . . .
>
> I wish it were the daily practice in every home of the Saints of God. If it were, we would be a much more

faithful people than we are today. (Conference Report, Oct. 1901, 14.)

ONE FAMILY'S SUCCESS

I have some friends who for many years were sporadic in having scripture reading with their children. They would do it for a while; then they'd quit. Then they'd start, and then they'd quit again. They would let obstacles get in their way. Their older sons grew up and got married, but they still had two daughters at home. Finally they got on track and began to consistently read with their family, day in and day out, without fail. Here is a set of letters they wrote me about their success:

The mother: "After a recent general conference, my husband and I talked about how we could start, once again, to have family scripture study on a regular basis. Conference had pricked our consciences—maybe I should say pierced them—and we knew it was the thing we should do. We decided to present the idea to our two daughters, one Primary age at the time and one a teenager, at our next family home evening. I was worried about how the girls were going to accept our proposal. One wasn't too fond of scripture reading, and both hated to get up early.

"We fasted and prayed to try to invite the Spirit to witness that what we were going to say was true. We also used the scriptures and quotes from President Benson's conference talk.

"I'm pleased to say that it went beautifully. We expressed our love to the girls, to our Father in Heaven, and the Savior. We told them we needed to repent of not having more consistent scripture study in our home. The Spirit that was there touched their hearts, and ours, as we bore testimony to the truthfulness of what we had said. The girls agreed, and we're now having scripture study early in the morning each day.

"We read very slowly and discuss each verse, looking at

how we can apply it in our lives. That is an important key. We're also trying very hard to have the Spirit each time we read. We realize that without the Spirit there to bear witness, real learning and doing will not take place.

"Our scripture reading has brought into our home a wonderful spirit of peace and love that was not there before. Before, our girls would often argue, talk disrespectfully, or be inconsiderate. Now they do much better. I also find myself being more patient and considerate. More importantly, our testimonies are growing, and there's a great desire and effort to live the gospel."

The younger daughter, age twelve: "The night my mom and dad gave us a lesson on how they had strong feelings we should start family scripture study, I knew immediately they were right. My eyes were all watering, and I felt warm inside. The Spirit came so strong to me that night, I was afraid if I heard one more word about it, I would burst into tears. I was eager to begin.

"Everything went smoothly the morning we began. We started at 6:00 A.M. Each morning I would be more reluctant about getting up. I liked reading the scriptures; I just hated getting up in the morning. Although I'm reluctant, I still go with the best attitude I've ever had because I know it will save our family from the outside world, and I know it is right!"

The older daughter, age fifteen: "For family home evening, my mom and dad fasted and prayed for the Spirit. They told us they wanted to repent for lacking enough spirituality in our home and family. They said they wanted to start having scripture study, so we planned to start the next week. It was hard getting up that early, but I finally got used to it.

"We read a little and discuss it. It makes me feel really good the whole day. Everything seems to go much better. I didn't think I'd be ready for school on time because the scriptures took up part of my getting-ready time, but I'm finding now that I get up a little bit earlier, and it puts me in a happy mood for the whole day.

"I went home from school that first day feeling really good about the neat thing we had started. I'm grateful for it now, and I'm thankful it has happened. It makes each day better than it would otherwise be."

The father: "We do not force anyone to attend, although strong encouragement is given. We sing a hymn promptly at 6:00 A.M. An important element of our success is that we are *studying* and *experiencing* scripture reading together—we're not simply reading the Book of Mormon. We're not attempting to complete the reading of the book or even a chapter, but instead we're attempting to have close family togetherness while we read a few pages. We're trying to relate Nephi's family to our family—their pride to the pride in our family; their murmuring to our murmuring; their family contention to ours; their faith to ours; their testimony of the importance of records to our needs and circumstance; their goodly family to what we want to have. We don't just try to know what the verses mean, or how to use the footnotes and cross-references, but more importantly we want to know how it all relates to us. What does it mean anyway? What do we observe at school, at work, in our own lives and in the lives of others, that relates to what we're reading?

"We always close with a family prayer, a hug, and a kiss. We never go over twenty minutes. It doesn't matter if we read one verse or one chapter. The most important element is spending this time together, sharing and having Heavenly Father and his words with us. So far, we feel successful and optimistic.

"We know each day and each week will offer more challenges, but we feel that we will be up to them because we are united, and all of us are now in tune to the good things that are taking place in our lives and our family relationships. What a tremendous influence the scriptures are having on us. There is surely no question that it is never too late to begin scripture reading with your family."

As this family testifies, daily family scripture reading will change your life—and it will change the lives of your children as well.

We must not let the obstacles to family scripture study get in our way. The blessings are too important. The costs of failure are potentially too great. Let us resolve to be diligent in this family responsibility and opportunity. The Lord will bless us as we do. That is his promise.

MAKING IT
WORK

I assume that by now you are convinced you ought to be reading the scriptures as a family. But how do you get started? How do you get off dead-center and get moving?

When we had a younger family we would read faithfully for a week or two, and then we would quit for a month. Then we'd suddenly wake up and say, "What have we been doing? We forgot scripture reading." We would start again and would go for a month straight with no misses. We'd all start thinking, "Finally, we've made this a tradition." Then we would go into a nose dive again for two more months.

I think many families have had this same experience. How do we get going and stay consistent? In this chapter I hope to give you some very practical ideas, gained from our experience and that of others, that will help you make family scripture reading a lifetime tradition.

MAKE THE COMMITMENT

In 1976 my wife and I were deeply touched by a man who preached, by the Spirit, of the importance of holding family scripture reading. We determined that very night that we would no longer fail to have regular scripture reading in our family. We agreed that we would do whatever it took to put that tradition in place in our home. We wanted to make scripture reading, joined with family prayer, as common to our children as having breakfast in the morning.

We decided to fast and pray about it, seeking help to approach it in the right way—and seeking the Lord's help in touching the hearts of our children. We also sought the Lord's help in preparing our own hearts. When we felt all was in readiness, we gathered our children together, bore testimony to them, and told them of the spirit we'd been feeling. We told them we wanted to repent of our neglect.

When our children heard our feelings, they were touched by the Spirit as well. They agreed, and we all committed, "We will begin."

From that day until this, more than twenty years have gone by. We have not read together every single day of that period—there have been days we have missed. But I am happy to say that such times have been rare. And I bear testimony that I know of no single thing that has blessed and changed my family more. I will forever be thankful for the impression that came that day that convinced my wife and me that we must act and not hold back any longer.

Making a firm commitment—that is the first step.

WHEN TO DO IT

When is the best time to read scriptures as a family? The answer to that question is actually quite simple: the best time is the time that works best for you. Of course, that varies from family to family. I have seen some families do it successfully at night. For us, mornings have worked best—in the evening too many of our older children are gone. But who's not at home at six or six-thirty in the morning?

In some areas, teenagers may have to get up very early to attend early morning seminary. If that's your situation, you may need to hold your reading in two sessions—perhaps one early, with Mom and Dad and teenagers, and another session later, with Mom and the younger kids.

Another nice thing about reading in the morning is that everyone is making a sacrifice together. You have to get up earlier than you probably otherwise would. You may all feel a little tired, and it may take a little work to get everyone going—but it starts your day off on the right foot. If you can have a spiritual experience together in the morning, and then launch the whole family off to school, to work, or wherever else they need to go, you've made a big difference in their day.

I had to smile at one of my older boys when he was getting ready to go on a mission, after years of getting up at 6:00 A.M. for family scripture reading. "I can hardly wait to get into the mission field," he said.

"Why is that?" I asked.

"So I can sleep in," he said. Arising at 6:30 A.M. was the mission rule at that time.

I think getting our children up in the morning teaches them how to get going early in the day, and the discipline of that may teach them some great lessons in addition to the actual practice of scripture reading.

But, again, there is no best time of day for all people. Choose the time that is best for you, so that you can bless and strengthen your family on a daily basis.

If you simply cannot find a time to read together, read this impressive statement by President John Taylor, and let it build in you a spirit of repentance.

> We frequently think a little more of a nice span of horses, or a nice wagon, or a favorite cow, and such things, than we do of God's work, as our boys sometimes get attached to a few marbles thinking that they are everything. They do not like to leave their marbles to obey father or mother, and God finds us about the same. We get

a few dollars, or a farm, and a little stock, and a few other things, and we cannot afford to neglect these. We cannot afford to take time to pray, nor to listen to the voice of Father, we are so busy playing marbles. . . . We are here to build up Zion, and to establish the kingdom of God. (*Journal of Discourses*, 22:219–20.)

GETTING THE CHILDREN TO COME

If you're reading in the morning, how do you get the children up? We have tried all sorts of things. We've tried waking them by singing to them. We've tried tickling them. (Not always the best idea, to tickle a sleeping child who doesn't want to be disturbed.) We've tried dragging them. (Not ever a good idea—it just causes resentment, and it doesn't work anyway.) We've tried rewarding them. (Usually doesn't work in the long term.) We've tried punishing them. (More resentment.) We've tried the guilt routine, saying at breakfast, "Well, where were you? We sure missed you this morning." (This makes the parent the sheriff or the enforcer, and it doesn't work in the long run.)

If those things don't work, what does?

We have used one approach for some time that has worked quite well with our younger children. This was suggested by our eleven-year-old daughter. "Dad, I know what you should do if the other kids don't come to scripture reading. If they can't get up they must be too tired. So they must be getting to bed too late. Maybe if they miss scriptures in the morning they should have to go to bed an hour earlier that night. That will help them be ready to go the next morning."

It was a simple approach, but it has helped us motivate our younger children to get up and join us for our early morning reading.

Motivation from Within

One problem with that approach, and with all the others that don't work, is that they provide a motivation that is external to the children. Much better is to come up with a motivation that works from inside the child.

One way to do that is to have a private interview with each child. Take him or her off alone with Dad and Mom and have a little talk. "How are you feeling about our scripture reading? How could we do better? What would you do differently?" Encourage your child to share his or her true feelings and to give honest suggestions.

Sometimes you will need to fast and pray for solutions. Once, early on, my wife fasted rather fervently for one of our daughters, who was struggling to join us consistently for scripture reading. But that wasn't all—she convinced the daughter to join her in the fast. That made all the difference.

"Why Don't We Pray Together?"

It can also help to have a private prayer of a parent with a child. Many times if you will pray to the Lord with your child, kneeling side by side and asking for strength and help in behalf of the struggling child, that experience alone will be enough to motivate the child to do better.

Once one of our teenage sons skipped two or three mornings in a row, and my wife and I were anxious about what to do. One morning when he wasn't there I had something very important I needed to talk to the family about. I remember feeling a little angry. "Why isn't he here? Let's go get him." I was tempted to march down the stairs, wake him up, and get him on his way to our scripture reading. Fortunately, I contained myself and didn't do it.

When he came up for breakfast, I felt touched spiritually to take him off alone to visit with him for a moment. (I'll just call him John.) I took him by the arm and we went together into the bedroom. I said, "John, I know you must really be concerned about something. You're worried aren't you?"

"Well, I am kind of worried about some things at school, Dad," he said.

"Why don't we pray together before you go?" We knelt down together, and I offered a prayer asking the Lord to bless my son and asking that he would remove his doubts and fears, replacing them with faith. I prayed that my son would really begin to pray without ceasing through the day, that he would pray for the Lord to bless him that things would work out in his life.

After we finished, he offered a prayer. When we stood up, there was a great feeling of love between us. I told him I loved him and hoped he would have a good day. He took off for school. Not a word was mentioned about scripture study.

His mother reported that when he came back that afternoon, the first thing he said was, "Mom, what can I do to help you?" He worked for her most of that afternoon. All evening he was in great spirits, getting along with the rest of the family very well. The next morning he was with us promptly at six o'clock for our scripture reading.

Again, not a single word had been said about his nonattendance, but something else more powerful had been done in showing love to him and in helping him feel the Spirit of the Lord. He knew what he was supposed to be doing. He didn't need to be told. And I was fortunate that at least on that occasion I had followed the impressions the Lord had given me.

Sharing Responsibility

Another solution we've tried that has worked very well was to simply place on the children the responsibility to be there at six o'clock in the morning. We bought every single child an alarm clock. One morning we bore testimony to them of the importance of scripture reading and of the Lord's desire that they join us. We said, "From here on out, Dad and Mom will not come to wake you up. We won't come down making noise or stirring around to wake you up. Whether you come or not will be up to you. You each have your clock. You'll need to be independent enough to set it for the right time and to get up and get going when it rings."

Some of the children have tested us by missing a day or two to see if we were going to intervene. When they saw that they truly were on their own, they have decided that they wanted to be there, and they have come.

Perhaps this approach would not work for all families, but it certainly has worked for us.

Finally, if we want our children to be self-motivated in attending scripture reading, we need to make sure it's good enough that they will want to be there. We need to make sure that we bring the Spirit into our homes for those minutes. We need to create a setting where they can come and bask in the love they feel there, where they won't want to miss the fun and the learning experience.

All of that is primarily the responsibility of the father and the mother. And if the parents can accomplish that, the children will want to come—and when they miss, they will feel sorry they missed. I bear testimony that that's true.

Caution: Don't Let the Gospel Be a Bargaining Chip

Sometimes parents are so intent on doing what's right with their children that they are unwise in their methods. I would like to issue a caution to parents: be careful that you never let the gospel or the Church be a source of conflict between you and your child. Don't let the Church or the gospel become some kind of a bargaining chip. If you do, it could do great damage to your child's testimony. Let me illustrate.

Once one of our sons began to miss scripture reading from time to time. Then he became upset at his dad and mom about something, and he announced, "I'm not even going to church." He was baiting us to say, "Well, son, you know you should go to church. You know better than that." We could have given him that talk, but would it have made any difference? No. He was trying to set up a power struggle with the Church in the middle. (Sometimes children will pick something that is sacred to you or means a lot to you and use it as a lever in the relationship, hoping to get their way in something. They know that they will thereby get your attention.)

We simply said, "You'll have to decide that, John. That's between you and the Lord."

"Okay, but I'm telling you, I'm not going to church."

"You'll just have to decide that, son. We're not discussing it. That's between you and the Lord. You go resolve it with him. You know what's right as well as we do. It's between you and him."

He stuck with his resolve for two consecutive Sundays, skipping out the first hour of the meeting to see what Dad and Mom would do. We did nothing. We just ignored his behavior and went on our way. When he saw that the gospel was not a bargaining chip, something he could use as a lever to get his way with us, he dropped it and returned to attending his meetings.

I repeat, do not let a gospel principle or the Church get between you and a child in some kind of a conflict. And that applies to scripture reading. Parents, be wise with how you deal with recalcitrant children.

WHERE TO READ TOGETHER

Where is the best place to hold family scripture reading? Some families have done it around the parents' bed; some have done it on the floor; some have done it at the breakfast table or perhaps the supper table. Some have done it at the table before any food has been served. Some have done it on the couch, snuggled in a blanket.

In our family, we've found it difficult to have a good study time if we're eating. It's hard to concentrate. You can't mark your books. You might get them dirty.

We have also found it difficult to have a good study time if family members are lounging on the floor or the bed—it's too hard to stay alert (especially at 6:00 A.M.)!

The key is to find a place that's conducive to learning, a place where everybody can be alert. Use the same place every day, and let it become sacred to you, a place where the Lord's Spirit can always be found. If you will do that, perhaps it doesn't matter where you are when you read.

WHAT TO READ

What should you read in scripture reading? Where should you start?

I strongly recommend that all families, particularly those with children, begin by reading the Book of Mormon. For the past twenty years we've spent most of our time in the Book of Mormon. Sometimes we've read the Doctrine and Covenants for a while, or the Bible, but we always end up in the Book of Mormon, because it was given as the instrument of conversion. If your objective is to try to convert your children to the Lord through the Spirit, I believe the Book of Mormon is by far the best way to do it. In addition, the Book of Mormon is usually easier for the littler ones to understand.

When we've read with children who are too young to read well, we've used the illustrated versions of the Book of Mormon.

Once when one of our boys was about five, I was holding him on my knee as I read to him from an illustrated Book of Mormon. After I had read the story about Nephi going into Jerusalem to get the brass plates, I thought I'd better check to see how well he understood it. "Son," I said, "tell me why you think Nephi had to go back into Jerusalem to get the plates."

He thought a minute, then said, "Well, Dad, I guess they didn't have anything else to eat on."

Oh no, I thought, what kind of a teacher are you? Here I had been talking about plates without even thinking that he was familiar with only one kind of plates!

SHOULD WE READ THROUGH OR READ BY TOPIC?

Should we start at the beginning of the book and then read all the way through, or should we read by topics?

It's probably a good idea to do both. Perhaps you will want to begin at the beginning and start reading—and then when you come across a topic that's particularly interesting to your family, spend one or more days or weeks searching out that subject.

Over the years we have been reading, we've repeatedly come upon passages about the last days, and the children have sometimes said, "Dad and Mom, what's really going to happen in the last days before the Lord comes?"

Our response: "Shall we stop what we're reading and spend a number of sessions really studying the last days?"

"Yes, that's what we should do."

They have always been excited to do a topical study of things they are deeply interested in.

Whether you are reading in order or by topic, be sure to use the footnotes as you go along. They will help you teach the children how to use the footnotes, the Topical Guide, and the Bible Dictionary.

APPLYING THE SCRIPTURES TO YOUR FAMILY

I once had a man tell me, "Hey, I've always read for mileage." It was his goal to read ten pages every night, no matter what. Some families have a goal to read a whole chapter a day, no matter what.

In our home, we have taken a different approach. It's our plan to read for a given time, usually twenty-five or thirty minutes, and not worry about the number of pages. Usually we will read and discuss two or three or four or seven verses—and that's all. We are not reading for mileage.

We are also not very interested in whether or not our children know the names of the sons of Alma or the details of the wars. Instead, we're interested that they start having deep feelings in their hearts about Alma. And the best way we have found to do that (while also keeping it interesting, so they will want to come) is to read only a few verses, then stop. Tell a story about the verses. Bear your testimony about the principles. Apply the verses to your family.

I can't say that it is never appropriate to read through the scriptures as fast as you can. But it has never seemed appropriate for our family. If you are going to try to hear the voice of the Lord and have a spiritual experience, you need to ponder every word and every phrase while you're reading. Those who take such an approach learn much more than those who do not.

This, then, is the process that works for us: Read slowly, stop, apply the verses to your family. Use a lot of examples and illustrations your children will understand. If you do that, you won't cover a lot of pages per week, but you will probably touch hearts a lot more consistently.

Another valuable way to apply the scriptures is to bring personal problems and family problems to family scripture reading. I am not talking about making reading time a "gripe session." Instead, remind family members of the problem and say, "Children, how are we going to solve this difficulty in our family? What do the scriptures say?" Then spend some time looking up and sharing pertinent passages. This approach will breathe life into your scripture reading because everyone will be interested and concerned about the common problem, and you can search together for a common solution.

HAVING VARIETY IN FAMILY SCRIPTURE READING

Variety in scripture reading is important, especially for younger children. We have tried a number of things to bring more variety to the experience, and I think each one has been valuable.

One thing we've tried is called "two-minute talks." In a two-minute talk, Dad or Mom can call on somebody and say, "John, please give us a two-minute talk on repentance." John will have a minute to collect his thoughts; then he has to stand up and bear his testimony and talk about repentance. "Okay, Mom, your turn. Humility, please. Two minutes." She has a minute to think, and then stands and begins to talk. Our two-minute talks are fun, and they put more life into our scripture reading experience.

Sometimes we have spent the whole time in a testimony meeting. That has been both fun and inspiring.

Sometimes we've had scripture chases to teach the children how to find things quickly in the various books of scripture. A nice side-effect: scripture chases wake everybody up in the morning.

Sometimes we spend our time memorizing. We have memorized the names of the books in the Bible, and we've memorized specific scriptures. This adds some variety to what we're doing, helps the children to be more alert, and at the same time teaches them some important things.

Sometimes we have spent the time sharing stories we like or sharing personal experiences, even if they are not directly related to the scriptures. Sometimes when I have come home from one of my trips the children will say, "Dad, tell us about what happened on the weekend." So I will give them a report of a special experience I had, or maybe I'll share with them the essence of a talk I gave. We may spend our entire scripture study time on such a report, with testimony, love, and some stories mingled into it.

Sometimes after the conference issue of the *Ensign* comes out, we stop reading the scriptures for a few weeks and read key general conference talks out loud to one another. Sometimes we assign one of the children to prepare a report on one of the talks. This enables us to hear the words of the living prophets as well as the ancient prophets.

Sometimes we have talked about other articles from the Church magazines, reviewing things that we feel are particularly pertinent or useful.

Sometimes when we have been pressed with a difficult day ahead, we've used our scripture study time to plan or schedule the day, or to listen to music. When the children were younger, on occasion we would even spend time marching around the house to loud music, just to wake everybody up.

Sometimes we will spend the time talking about important current events, which we will then relate to the gospel.

But even though we try to put some variety into our time together, we still spend most of the time (probably 90 percent) studying the scriptures. The variety helps to keep everyone interested—especially when children are younger—but don't forget to keep your focus on the scriptures.

USING TAPES AND PICTURE BOOKS

Another way to add variety to your reading, if you have younger children, is to use picture books and tapes. Here is one family's experience with these helpful tools:

> Several years ago we were vacationing with friends who were living in Mexico. We were quite impressed

when we witnessed first hand what they were able to accomplish spiritually with their children.

We participated with this sweet family every morning for a week in their early morning devotional and scripture study. They began with a song and ended with a family prayer. Because their children were young, their scripture study utilized *Book of Mormon Stories* and the accompanying tapes published and produced by the Church. Everyone listened to the tape and followed along with the pictures in the book. Sometimes they stopped the tape to have a discussion. Other times they had a discussion at the end of the "chapter." The pictures allowed the scriptures to come alive for the children. I think the discussion led by the parents was of the greatest value. The spirit that was in their home was so incredibly strong that we wanted that same spirit in our home.

When we returned home to our three young children, we dedicated ourselves to trying to duplicate what we had seen our friends do. Since our children were also very young, we purchased the audiocassettes and a separate copy of the scripture reader book for each member of the family, including Mom and Dad. We started with *Book of Mormon Stories,* then went to *New Testament Stories* and the others in the series. We did this for several years, rotating through each book of scripture stories.

Sometimes we would stop the tape in the middle and discuss what was happening. We would express our feelings about the faith of Nephi or the courage of Abinadi. Or we would bear our testimony about how we felt as we listened to the tape. Because each picture was referenced to a scripture, whenever we wanted to we could easily look up a verse or two in the actual text of the scriptures. We could then read and comment on it or underline it in our scriptures.

We found that by using the cassettes and pictures our small children were able to get a lot from the scriptures. We sometimes even discovered our children going over the pictures in the book on their own later in the day. Our years with the picture books made it easier for our children to start reading the actual text when they grew older.

Our youngest child, Andrew, is eight years younger than the rest of the children. By the time he began to participate with us in scripture reading, we were reading the actual text of the scriptures. But, for Andrew's sake, we went back to the pictures and cassette tapes. The older children didn't seem to mind that the content was directed to a younger set. They were able to participate in sharing their feelings with us and their younger brother.

We feel that understanding is more important than just getting done, so we have always spent time discussing what we read or listened to. Children need to hear how Mom and Dad feel about the scriptures and the gospel. Also, encouraging the children to ask questions helps them clarify and understand things on their own level.

Over the years we've had several Primary and Sunday School teachers comment to us that our children seemed to know the gospel and the scripture stories quite well. We attributed this to our family scripture study. More important, I feel our children love the Lord and feel the scriptures are a blessing in their lives.

Every family appears to have its ups and downs. It seems easier to have family scripture study during the school year when there is a daily routine in the kids' lives. But we have learned to take the scriptures on family vacations and read together then.

We can testify that the best times in our family, the times when we have felt the Spirit the most, are when we have been having family scripture study and family home evening. It has greatly influenced our family and our testimonies of the Savior.

"OUR ROUGH EDGES ARE SMOOTHED"—A SUCCESS STORY

As I have talked with people about family scripture reading, many have shared their successes with me. Here is an experience written by one sister whose family persisted through special challenges and succeeded in their efforts to be consistent in their scripture reading.

I believe that regular scripture study is one of the best things we can do for our families, even though it might be a struggle each time! An additional challenge our family has is that my husband is not a member of the Church and does not join us for scripture study or family prayer. Because of this, it has always been up to me to call our three daughters together for scripture study. (However, my husband *has* occasionally nudged us along. Since we have found the best time for our family is just before bedtime, if he wants to hurry everyone to bed he sometimes reminds us to get started, which I do appreciate!)

Even though I have always recognized the importance of scripture reading as a family, taking the time for it has always been my biggest challenge. Until the girls were ages seven, four, and three, our scripture study consisted mainly of occasionally telling scripture stories on Sunday and Wednesday nights. We were pretty successful with this for awhile.

Then President Benson gave us a challenge to read the Book of Mormon together on a regular basis. This really had an impact on me, and I felt we should follow the prophet. I talked to the girls, and they agreed to read the Book of Mormon together as a family during the year.

Since they were not old enough to read along with me, at least not well, I would read to them each night. I must admit to sometimes putting the scriptures into my own words, occasionally leaving out "And it came to pass" and replacing it with "Then," and generally trying to make it more understandable. It was slow going, and with the girls misbehaving at times it was often discouraging, but luckily the Lord provided some immediate blessings to encourage us.

Blessings from the Lord

First, on the days we read scriptures, we noticed that the contention level around the house decreased dramatically. Even my girls noticed the difference. Another positive aspect of scripture reading was that it brought our day-to-day living to a more spiritual level. It gave us eternal perspective. It was interesting to see how much more often we would talk about spiritual things, even if it was just looking at a beautiful sunset or a rainbow and expressing how grateful we were to Heavenly Father for this beautiful world. There were also moments when we felt the Spirit very strongly as we read. With all these blessings, we reached our goal of reading the entire Book of Mormon that year and felt we had really accomplished something!

After that first year, we all had a stronger testimony of scripture reading. And with that experience as a foundation, I wish I could say that it became easier and less discouraging and that we have faithfully read the scriptures on a regular basis ever since. But, unfortunately, we still sometimes went for months on end without reading. It's amazing how quickly a few nights of not reading the scriptures turns into weeks and months. Usually, though, after listening to a conference talk or a speaker in sacrament meeting, we would get motivated and start again. How grateful I am that the Lord has patience and doesn't give up on us!

During the last four or five years we have been fairly regular in our studying, coupled with a family prayer at the end. We've missed a week or two here or there, but instead of making excuses or feeling guilty, we jump right back into it. Even though we rarely make our goal of reading seven nights a week, we do read the scriptures at least three to five times a week.

What Has Worked for Us

We have found that reading straight through the scriptures has worked best for us. Sometimes we read only a few verses. Other times we read several chapters. When my oldest daughter began seminary a few years ago, we decided to read the Doctrine and Covenants, which is what her class was studying. Later, however, we heard a conference talk that said we should be reading the Book of Mormon with our families every day. So we decided we would do both.

Unfortunately, it didn't work. The girls complained they couldn't keep the books straight. So we went back to reading the Book of Mormon. As a result, we haven't done much family reading in other books of scripture, but I'm holding fast to the prophet's promise that our family will be blessed as we continue to read the Book of Mormon.

We've also discovered that our daughters are too competitive to take turns reading in the same night. Trying to go around in a circle only made the girl who was reading complain that her verse was too long or two short, or it made her sisters complain that she was reading too slow or too fast. In addition, they were so busy trying to keep track of their next scripture that they weren't listening to what was being read.

About a year ago they asked if I would read while they listened and followed along. They said that when they read aloud they were so busy concentrating on pronouncing words correctly that they didn't understand what they had just read. So that is what we do now. They seem to understand it better, and we've had some wonderful gospel discussions relating to what we're reading. They've asked great questions, which shows they are listening. Sometimes the best moments come when I ask them to relate how the passage can apply to their lives, or to share a personal experience with the gospel principle we are studying.

"THEY LEARNED THE LANGUAGE OF THE SCRIPTURES"

One Family's Experience

"Our desire for our children was to instill within them the same love for the scriptures we have and to teach them how to go to the scriptures for answers to life's questions.

"We started studying as a family when our children were babies. We used illustrated versions of the standard works and told them the stories as we explained the pictures. By the time they were three or four, they each had their

Sometimes as we are reading, the girls will ask a gospel question that doesn't relate to what we are reading. Depending on the question, I ask them to wait until we are finished reading to discuss it, or if it seems particularly important, we stop and discuss it right then. Of course, those wonderful gospel discussions don't happen often.

More commonly, I'm afraid, one of the girls asks us to hurry, saying she has to finish her homework or make a phone call, and her barely concealed impatience makes it own set of scriptures. They would sit on our laps and, when it was their turn, we would read a verse while they repeated after us. In this way they learned the language of the scriptures and learned to relate them to the stories they heard in Primary. We had a goal that both our children would complete the Book of Mormon before their baptisms, which they both accomplished.

"Later, we changed our format. We would have one child read a few verses, then would ask another family member to explain it or 'liken it unto us.' We also tried taking turns reading and explaining favorite verses instead of reading verse by verse. Another approach we tried was having each person choose a scripture hero and use the scriptures to explain that hero's qualities. For even more variety, we have followed the footnote trails and have studied by subjects, marking as we've gone along. At other times we simply read verse by verse. We have found that occasional variety is a key to keeping our children excited about family scripture study. Our next phase of study will be to search during the week for scriptures that relate to our family home evening lesson."

hard to have a quality scripture time. But I have to keep reminding myself that the good experiences would never have happened if we hadn't been reading, so we keep trying.

Is It Worth It?

When the girls are especially giggly or are pretending to sleep or are reluctant to take the time to read, I sometimes ask myself: "Is it worth the effort?" The answer is YES! I feel that each time we read the scriptures it has a positive effect on my children, whether they are aware of it or not. A couple of my daughters have even started reading scriptures on their own each night, in addition to our family scripture study. Each one has told me privately, "Mom, I just can't sleep until I've done my reading." How grateful I am that the habit of regular study has influenced their lives! I've seen it in the choices they've made, the friends they have, and the sincere repenting they've done when mistakes have been made.

Regular scripture reading reminds me of the beautifully rounded, smooth stones that can be found in the Northwest, where we have many streams, rivers, and ocean beaches. As a child, I loved picking them up and collecting them. I marveled at how, through eons of time, the gentle, constant action of the waves could take away the rough edges and make them so beautifully rounded and smooth. That is how I feel the scriptures work on us. It is my testimony that through the constant, gentle action of reading and studying them, our rough edges are smoothed away, we become well-rounded in the gospel, and our souls become more beautiful, more like our Savior, Jesus Christ.

CHAPTER 16

STRENGTHENING YOUR FAMILY SCRIPTURE STUDY

(A SUGGESTED FORMAT)

Once when I was presenting these ideas in a fireside, we took some time and worked through a role play of a family reading scriptures together. It proved to be so helpful that I am reproducing the experience here. What follows is an edited transcript of an actual role play. Present are Dad, Mom, Alan (age eighteen), Sarah (age thirteen), and Nate (age eleven). The family is gathered in the living room, seated and trying to be alert. It is 6:00 A.M. Each person has a copy of the Book of Mormon and a pencil to mark with.

Dad: Well, family, how are you this morning?

Sarah: Tired.

Dad: It's hard getting going sometimes, isn't it? But I'm sure glad to see you all here this morning. It sure means a lot to me and your mom to see how good you children are. We want you to know we love you, all of you.

Children:. We love you, too.

Mom: For our song this morning, let's sing a verse of "I Am a Child of God." Everybody ready? Here we go.

Everybody: "I am a child of God, and he has sent me here . . ."

Mom: Thanks, everybody. Now let's sing a verse of that song Nate likes so much, "Jesus Said Love Everyone."

Everybody: "Jesus said love everyone; treat them kindly, too . . ."

Dad: That's great. I'll offer the morning prayer today. *[All bow their heads. Dad prays that the Lord will bless the family that morning, that they will be awake both physically and spiritually. He asks that the Lord will open their hearts, that they will be humble, that they might feel love toward one another, and that the Spirit will be present and will be felt in their reading time together. He asks that if the Lord has a special message of some kind for the family, he will help family members to open their minds to it. He expresses love for the Lord and for the members of his family and expresses gratitude that each person is a member of the family.]*

Dad: Now, where were we in our reading?

Nate: Alma 37, verse 6.

Dad: Thanks, Nate. Yesterday we were talking about how the plates were preserved, and the Lord said they'd end up going to all the nations. In verse five he promised that they would always retain their brightness. Remember that? Now, Nate, would you start us off for today with verse six?

Nate: "Now ye may suppose that this is foolishness in me; but behold I say unto you, that by small and simple things are great things brought to pass; and small means in many instances doth confound the wise. And the Lord God doth work by means to bring about his great and eternal purposes; and by very small means the Lord doth confound the wise and bringeth about the salvation of many souls." Now, Sarah, will you explain it?

Sarah: It means that if we try to be wise without the Lord, he will confound us. And maybe that the Lord will use small and simple things to bring to pass great miracles.

Alan: I like that idea, too. I think it's neat that the Lord uses simple ways to do his work, not big, fancy ways.

Dad: Yes, he uses such simple methods that if you're not careful, you won't even know he did anything. I've often thought about that quality of God when I think of how he told *us* to be anonymous givers. You know what that means, Nate?

Nate: Not for sure.

Dad: It means that you do things in secret for people so they never know who did the good thing for them. Can you see that the Lord is probably the best secret giver of all? Like Mom says, if you're not careful, he'll do a lot of good to you and you'll never even know it, because he does so much without taking credit for it. Nate, since you read, remember you need to ask the family a question about that verse.

Nate: Yeah. My question is, "What does it mean 'and small means in many instances doth confound the wise'?"

Dad: Good question. Who can answer that?

Alan: Well, I think he means that the Lord uses small things to do his work—like maybe us reading scriptures together—but they're so small that people who think they are wise don't understand how it can affect a family.

Dad: That's good, Alan. I think that's exactly right.

Mom: Let me give you another example. You children know Alan will be going on a mission in another year. And some people who think they are wise might say, "Well, what could a young man like Alan do out in the mission field? Why doesn't the Lord send out older men and women who have a lot more experience and leave the nineteen-year-olds at home?" Sending out young, inexperienced men is such a small and simple thing. What can one young man accomplish? But Alan will go out and teach people and touch many lives. He'll baptize people into the true Church and kingdom of God. Maybe he'll baptize ten, or maybe a hundred, or maybe three hundred, depending on where he's called to serve. And those people will have children or grandchildren who will come into the Church. Before long, there will be enough new members from Alan's missionary service to form a branch, or a ward, or a stake, if they all lived in the same place. Can you see how the Lord can use a small, simple thing like sending a young man on a mission to bring about the salvation of many people?

Dad: Thanks, Mom. Anybody else want to make a comment? Okay, Nate, who did you call on to explain the verse you read?

Nate: Sarah.

Dad: Oh, that's right. Sarah. I guess it's your turn.

Sarah: "And now, it has hitherto been wisdom in God that these things should be preserved; for behold, they have enlarged the memory of this people, yea, and convinced many of the error of their ways, and brought them to the knowledge of their God unto the salvation of their souls." Alan, your turn to explain the verse, please.

Alan: This verse shows that the scriptures help us know what we're doing wrong. People need to change so they can come closer to Heavenly Father and have salvation. I think it shows the importance of the scriptures.

Mom: Thanks, Alan. I noticed something else in this verse that's important, in the beginning of the verse, where it says that these things should be preserved. Sarah, what do you think he's talking about when he says "these things"?

Sarah: Are they the scriptures?

Dad: Exactly. It's the plates or the scriptures, isn't it? He's saying they're going to be preserved. Now, you know we've talked in the family a lot about marking the scriptures, haven't we. This verse gives us three things the scriptures do for us. Why don't you get your pencils and mark with me? See in verse 8 where it says that "they," meaning the scriptures, "have enlarged the memory of this people"? I'd put a "1" in the margin there. Then put a "2" in the margin where it says, " . . . yea, and convinced many of the error of their ways." Then see where it says, " . . . brought them to the knowledge of their God unto the salvation of their souls"? I'd put a "3" there. It's a great little list of blessings we get from the scriptures.

Mom: I really like that. So the scriptures will enlarge your memory. Isn't that amazing? Have you ever thought about that before? Your dad and I really need help with that, don't we? But, really, I know it's true. The more we study, the more I see that the Lord can bring back to our minds things we've learned or known or experienced in the past. He can even help us remember truths we knew before we came to this life, before the veil was over our minds. And, second, it says the scriptures will convince many of the error of their ways, even me. Does it mean that?

Nate: Yup.

Mom: Sure it does. So maybe if I'm not as patient as I should be, or if I'm not humble enough, the scriptures will help me know the error of my ways. They will tell you the things you need to know so you can repent. Now, children, let's apply this to ourselves in a very direct way. Do we have any areas in our family where we're in error?

Alan: Well, I think we've all been guilty of fighting and squabbling with each other. There's too much teasing and contention sometimes. Maybe reading these scriptures will help us understand that this is not what we want in our home.

Mom: You all know I feel the same way. Why don't we talk about that for a minute? What could we do to have more peace in our home? Alan, would you get a sheet of paper so we can write down what we decide to do? *[Family discussion follows.]*

Dad: Children, let's really try to do better on this. It's so important for us to have the Spirit of the Lord in our home, and contention drives the Spirit away. Now, Nate, what's the third thing Alma says the scriptures will do?

Nate: It brought them to the knowledge of their God.

Dad: Right. Are the scriptures bringing our family to the knowledge of God, Sarah?

Sarah: Yes, they are.

Dad: They are. And I bear testimony to you, family, that the Lord is seeing us converted more and more as we read here together every morning. Have you noticed that? He is bringing to our understanding the knowledge of God, and as he says, it will save our own souls. I bear testimony to you, children, that your mom and I love you very much. You're a great family. And I bear witness that if we'll continue doing this faithfully every day, the Lord will bring about an even greater conversion of every one of us in this circle. I want you to know that, and that I love you for getting up in the mornings and making the effort to come to our family scripture time. Thank you for all that you are.

Well, we had better conclude. But before we do, I need to ask, What is the most important thing you've felt today in scripture reading, or the most important thing you've learned?

Sarah: I've felt that if we keep reading the scriptures like this, and if we really try, we'll be able to have a lot happier home.

Alan: That's what I've been thinking. If we can just feel the Spirit each morning when we spend this time, and then try to keep it, we'll be able to get along better and have more harmony in our home.

Mom: And it doesn't have to be a big deal. The Lord will use that small means to bring to pass large blessings.

Nate: I like the part about the Lord being the best secret giver ever. I think that's neat.

Dad: Great answers, everyone. Let's have our closing prayer.

[Family kneels. In the opening prayer the family asked for inspiration and enlightenment. In the closing prayer, they might thank the Lord for the Spirit they have enjoyed, for a wonderful family, and for the privilege of spending time together and learning from the Lord.]

After the Prayer

In our home, after we say "Amen" we throw our arms around every other member of the family, each in turn, and say "I love you. I love you." It's a simple thing, yet it seems to put a final seal of love on the time we spend together worshipping the Lord in our family scripture reading.

Sometimes our discussions carry right over into breakfast. We continue to talk about what we have learned, and it's a great blessing to the entire family.

(It would probably be appropriate to say a word here about our practice in our evening family prayer. This is not a recommendation for others but simply an example of an approach that's been a blessing for us. After the family has knelt, we prepare ourselves to pray by singing a verse of a hymn. That helps quiet the children down and get us more into the reverent mood we want for our prayer. Or maybe I'll say, "Okay, John, it's your turn, and Mom's." That means that John and Mom both have to recite a scripture they have memorized. Or they might recite an Article of Faith. Every week or two we try to learn a new scripture, so periodically, before prayer, we will take a minute to recite what we've learned, which will help us to make it more a part of our lives. I have been amazed at the confidence and spiritual maturity that come to the children as they memorize and quote out loud the words of the Lord.)

Lessons from the Role Play

As we think about the role play, what did this family do to bring the Spirit of the Lord into their meeting? How did the parents approach things so that the family could learn from the Lord and not just from the words on the page? Here are a few ideas from the role-play experience that can help each of us in our family scripture reading:

• The meeting began with a song and a prayer. Sometimes two opening songs are necessary, to wake family members up more. The prayer was specific and asked for the needs of the hour—to have the presence of the Spirit and to understand the scriptures. If the father (or mother if she is a single parent) thinks the child assigned to pray may not remember to pray specifically, the parent can say, "Nate, be sure to remember to ask the Lord to specifically help us understand and be humble, would you please?"

• The father took time at both the beginning and the end of the family devotional to express love and gratitude to family members. Sometimes in the Cook home we take this a step further. We might start a scripture reading time with each of us saying one thing we love most about Alan, for example. That's a sweet moment, a moment that will bind your family together in love.

• Each person had his or her own scriptures and marking pencils or pens.

• The father presided and took the lead of the meeting. At the same time the wife contributed freely and had much to add. The ultimate objective is to get the children to say more and more as they grow, while the parents say less and less.

• There was great love in the family, both expressed outwardly and displayed without words. When that love is there, you don't have to labor with the children to get them to come to scripture reading time. They'll be like bees coming to a hive. They will simply *want* to be there.

• The parents involved everybody. It is important that dad and mom don't dominate too much—but they will still want to direct the experience so each child will understand what's being discussed. Each person was involved, in turn, in reading, asking questions, and calling on someone else to read.

The family in the role play followed a procedure that has

worked well in our family for years. Let me outline it to make it clear:

1. We have one person read a verse or two.

2. The person who read then calls on another family member, without notice, to explain what was read. That helps everyone pay attention.

3. Next, the rest of the family can comment on the verse.

4. Then the person who read has to generate a question out of the verse. Why is that important? It helps us to see the scriptures as an answer book. We learn much more from the scriptures when we ask questions and try to connect them to the answers we are reading.

5. Finally, the one who just explained the verse becomes the next reader. (When you simply read straight through, family members tend to look ahead to see when their next turn is—and they may not pay as much attention until it is their turn again.)

• When the family in the role play found a passage that needed some marking, they stopped right there and did it. That helped them take full advantage of the reading experience.

• The parents bore testimony to the truthfulness of the points as they went along. The dad might bear testimony, or the mom, or in the spirit of involvement Dad might call on any one of the children.

• The parents applied the verses to themselves and to the family. They sought to know what the Lord would have them understand about it all. In the role play, the family discussed ways to diminish contention in the home. If you can get a good discussion on things that really matter, that makes the whole reading time worth it, even if you read only one verse. Remember, the objective is to get the messages of the scriptures into the hearts of the children, not just to get mileage by reading through.

CHAPTER 17

BRINGING THE SPIRIT
TO YOUR TIME TOGETHER

One of a parent's greatest challenges in scripture reading is to make sure that the Spirit is present in abundance. But we don't have to just *hope*. There are things we can do that will help us to consistently have the Spirit of the Lord in our homes, especially during scripture reading time. And if we have that Spirit, both the parents and children can be touched, blessed, and changed—and each family member can be strengthened every day we read the words of the Lord together.

This chapter, then, focuses on seven scriptural performances (see Alma 31:10) that, if humbly employed, will immediately invite the Spirit into your heart and the hearts of your children. We have talked about many of these in another context elsewhere in the book, but share them here in the context of bringing the Spirit into your home.

1. PRAY

Pray for the Spirit. Pray in the beginning of your scripture reading; pray at the end of your scripture reading; and ask each family member to maintain a prayerful heart while you are reading together.

I remember once while we were reading together there was a spirit of contention in the room. After putting up with it for about five minutes, my wife and I finally said, "Hey, this isn't working. Come on, family, let's kneel down again, and this time let's really pray to the Lord." Just that simple act of humbling ourselves and asking for the Spirit brought it into our home— and brought a blessing that otherwise would have been lost.

All your prayers don't have to be formal, kneeling prayers, of course. If one of your children creates problems during scripture reading, pray silently in your heart for him or her. That has real power, and the results will be readily apparent.

At the same time, pray for understanding. As the Lord said to the Nephites:

> I perceive that ye are weak, that ye cannot understand all my words which I am commanded of the Father to speak unto you at this time.
>
> Therefore, go ye unto your homes, and ponder upon the things which I have said, and ask of the Father, in my name, that ye may understand, and prepare your minds for the morrow, and I come unto you again. (3 Ne. 17:2–3.)

2. Use the Scriptures

As we have emphasized, the scriptures are the words of the Lord to us, and the Spirit of the Lord will speak through them to all, young and old. (See 2 Ne. 32:3; Alma 31:5; D&C 32:4.) If you want to have the Spirit of the Lord in your family gathering to read the scriptures, use the scriptures. That is not as paradoxical as it sounds. If a problem comes up, specifically relate it to a passage in the scriptures. It is always a blessing if you can apply a particular passage to a specific difficulty or to something that is happening at that very moment in your family.

This suggestion falls under the category of "When all else fails, read the instructions." The scriptures truly are the Lord's instructions to us, and he will bless us as we seek to use them in specific ways to bless our families.

I find the account in Alma to be a great motivation to use this principle:

> And now, as the preaching of the word had a great tendency to lead the people to do that which was just— yea, it had had more powerful effect upon the minds of the people than the sword, or anything else, which had happened unto them—therefore Alma thought it was expedient that they should try the virtue of the word of God. (Alma 31:5.)

3. TESTIFY

I don't believe we have ever read the scriptures together without sharing testimony. Parents, testify constantly. Teach and then testify. Testimony is what will carry your words to the hearts of your children. (See 2 Ne. 33:1.) Remember the experience I had with President Joseph Fielding Smith—his testimony blessed me that day, and it continues to bless me to this day. You can provide such a blessing to your children as well.

When Alma left the judgment seat, he went forth to teach and to reclaim his people.

> And this he did that he himself might go forth among his people, or among the people of Nephi, that he might preach the word of God unto them, to stir them up in remembrance of their duty, and that he might pull down, by the word of God, all the pride and craftiness and all the contentions which were among his people, seeing no way that he might reclaim them save it were in bearing down in pure testimony against them. (Alma 4:19.)

In the chapter that follows, we have the words he taught and testified among the people on that occasion. His testimony is itself a profound witness of the power of testifying:

"I GOT
A WARM FEELING"

*The Testimony of
a Young Boy*

"My name is Michael. I am eight years old. I read the Book of Mormon with my family. We read the promise. I prayed one night and I woke up in the night and remembered the Book of Mormon and I got a warm feeling about it that it was true."

I am commanded to stand and testify unto this people the things which have been spoken by our fathers concerning the things which are to come.

And this is not all. Do ye not suppose that I know of these things myself? Behold, I testify unto you that I do know that these things whereof I have spoken are true. And how do ye suppose that I know of their surety?

Behold, I say unto you they are made known unto me by the Holy Spirit of God. Behold, I have fasted and prayed many days that I might know these things of myself. And now I do know of myself that they are true; for the Lord God hath made them manifest unto me by his Holy Spirit; and this is the spirit of revelation which is in me.

And moreover, I say unto you that it has thus been revealed unto me, that the words which have been spoken by our fathers are true, even so according to the spirit of prophecy which is in me, which is also by the manifestation of the Spirit of God.

I say unto you, that I know of myself that whatsoever I shall say unto you, concerning that which is to come, is true; and I say unto you, that I know that Jesus Christ shall come, yea, the Son, the Only Begotten of the Father, full of grace, and mercy, and truth. And behold, it is he that cometh to

take away the sins of the world, yea, the sins of every man
who steadfastly believeth on his name. (Alma 5:44–48.)

4. USE MUSIC

Music will bring the Spirit of the Lord very quickly.
Sometimes early in the mornings we play some beautiful music
on a cassette and let it resound through our home at scripture
reading time, and that has worked wonderfully well. In addition,
as a matter of course, we sing the hymns of Zion and Primary
songs. These things do much to help bring the Spirit of the Lord.

As we get ready for family prayer, we have found that the
Primary songs are particularly powerful—they're easy, they're
short, and they have a clear and important message. Plus, little
children usually know them (and adults can learn)!

Paul wrote in counsel to the Colossians,

> Let the word of Christ dwell in you richly in all wis-
> dom; teaching and admonishing one another in psalms
> and hymns and spiritual songs, singing with grace in your
> hearts to the Lord. (Col. 3:16.)

And in our day the Lord said,

> For my soul delighteth in the song of the heart; yea, the
> song of the righteous is a prayer unto me, and it shall be
> answered with a blessing upon their heads. (D&C 25:12.)

5. EXPRESS LOVE AND
GRATITUDE TO GOD AND MAN

If you want to bring the Spirit into your scripture study,
express love to God, in front of your family, and to man, meaning to your wife and your children. Do it humbly and sincerely,
and the Spirit of the Lord will immediately come.

When Nephi was experiencing his wonderful vision of the

tree of life, the angel explained that the tree "is the love of God, which sheddeth itself abroad in the hearts of the children of men; wherefore, it is the most desirable above all things. . . . Yea, and the most joyous to the soul." (1 Ne. 11:22–23.) (And what led to that love, represented by the tree? The word of God, which was represented by the rod of iron!)

When we can sincerely offer love to our children, they will be drawn to us, and the Spirit of the Lord will be present. After all, we are offering something that, in its perfect form, "is the most desirable above all things" and "the most joyous to the soul."

6. SHARE A SPIRITUAL EXPERIENCE

As appropriate, be quick to share a spiritual experience that applies to something you have just read. If you use spiritual examples from your own life, you will invite the Spirit into your home and will help bring about the conversion of all present.

We see a classic example of this principle—and its power—in Paul's testimony to King Agrippa:

> My manner of life from my youth, which was at the first among mine own nation at Jerusalem, know all the Jews;
>
> Which knew me from the beginning, if they would testify, that after the most straitest sect of our religion I lived a Pharisee. . . .
>
> I verily thought with myself, that I ought to do many things contrary to the name of Jesus of Nazareth.
>
> Which thing I also did in Jerusalem: and many of the saints did I shut up in prison, having received authority from the chief priests; and when they were put to death, I gave my voice against them. . . .
>
> Whereupon as I went to Damascus with authority and commission from the chief priests,
>
> At midday, O king, I saw in the way a light from

heaven, above the brightness of the sun, shining round about me and them which journeyed with me.

And when we were all fallen to the earth, I heard a voice speaking unto me, and saying in the Hebrew tongue, Saul, Saul, why persecutest thou me? it is hard for thee to kick against the pricks.

And I said, Who art thou, Lord? And he said, I am Jesus whom thou persecutest.

But rise, and stand upon thy feet: for I have appeared unto thee for this purpose, to make thee a minister and a witness both of these things which thou hast seen, and of those things in the which I will appear unto thee. . . .

Having therefore obtained help of God, I continue unto this day, witnessing both to small and great, saying none other things than those which the prophets and Moses did say should come:

That Christ should suffer, and that he should be the first that should rise from the dead, and should shew light unto the people, and to the Gentiles. . . .

King Agrippa, believest thou the prophets? I know that thou believest.

Then Agrippa said unto Paul, Almost thou persuadest me to be a Christian. (Acts 26:4–5, 9–10, 12–16, 22–23, 27–28.)

7. PROVIDE PRIESTHOOD BLESSINGS

It may be that one or more members of your family is earnestly struggling to understand. Maybe his faith is a little weak. Maybe she doesn't like getting up in the morning. Whatever the problem, it may be appropriate to provide a priesthood blessing to that individual. As you do, it will help him or her receive the Spirit of the Lord—which will bless the family as a whole and enrich your scripture reading experience.

"In the ordinances" of the priesthood, the Lord said, "the power of godliness is manifest." (D&C 84:20.)

A PATTERN FOR HEARING THE VOICE OF THE LORD, APPLIED TO FAMILIES

In Part 2 we discussed a pattern for hearing the voice of the Lord, applied to our individual scripture studies. How might a family work together to try to apply that pattern? Let's review it here to see how it can work in a family setting:

1. Pray in faith. Family scripture reading will be a much greater blessing if the family begins and ends with prayer. The prayer should be specific, asking for help during the scripture reading time, and it should specifically ask for the Spirit to be present.

2. Humble yourself. Parents can teach their children to be humble during scripture reading time—and can set an example of humility themselves. One way we show that we're humble is to let ourselves be teachable—even if parents are being taught by their children.

3. Search diligently by pondering. Parents can teach their children the great value of pondering what they read in the scriptures. Parents can share with children the kinds of things they're pondering and what they're learning.

4. Search diligently by asking questions. As shown in the role play, this can be incorporated into the reading experience. I believe the more questions you ask as you read through the scriptures, the more you will be able to understand what's really there—and the more you will be able to apply it to yourself.

5. Search diligently by discovering patterns. This, too, can be incorporated into the family reading experience. If you're able to become familiar with the different kinds of patterns discussed earlier, you will then be able to spot them frequently as you read through the scriptures. Parents can point such patterns

out to their children—and, as the children grow in their understanding, they will be able to point them out for the family as well.

6. Search diligently by marking and cross-referencing. Children can learn much about these skills by practicing them as the family proceeds through the scriptures. Parents can suggest things to mark and ways to mark them.

7. Search diligently by applying the scriptures to yourself. Again, parents can teach this mindset and help the children practice from day to day as the family reads together. Parents can share the kinds of things they're working on in their lives and explain how the scriptures help them with their challenges.

8. Obey truths learned by repenting and changing. When the Lord teaches us what we are doing wrong, or failing to do right, we need to quickly

Preparing to Receive and Teach by the Spirit

The following is a summary of the suggestions in this chapter that will help you prepare yourself to teach by the Spirit—and at the same time prepare your family members to receive by that same Spirit.

1. Pray. Invite the Spirit to help you as you prepare to teach your family. Ask to better understand the needs of your children so you can say what the Lord would have you say. Ask family members to pray for you and for themselves while you teach. (See 3 Ne. 17:2–3; 20:1; D&C 136:29, 32.)

2. Use the scriptures. They are the words of the Lord to us, and the Spirit of the Lord will speak through them to all, young and old. (See 2 Ne. 32:3; Alma 31:5; D&C 32:4.)

3. Testify. If you follow his

resolve that we will follow his promptings and make a change. Reading the scriptures consistently will help us in that resolve, both by reinforcing our desire and by strengthening us with his Spirit. As we do repent and change, we'll be putting ourselves into a position where we can receive more light.

promptings, the Lord will direct you to testify frequently to his children. As you do so, the message will be transmitted to them by the Spirit, having a more powerful effect on their hearts than anything else. (See 2 Ne. 33:1; Alma 4:19; 5:44–47.)

4. Use music. When you are prompted, sing the songs of Zion, especially those about the Savior and his atoning sacrifice. Help your family concentrate on the messages as you sing the hymns together. (See 1 Sam. 16:23; Matt. 26:30; Col. 3:16; D&C 25:12.)

5. Express love and gratitude to God and man. Let each family member know that you love the Lord and them. Testify and express love openly for God and for them, and they will feel the Spirit because of your love for them. (See John 13:34–35; 1 Ne. 11:21–23; Moro. 7:47–48.)

6. Share spiritual experiences as appropriate. Gospel principles that are received spiritually are permanently impressed upon the soul. Share, as appropriate, your own experiences and the experiences of others that have had a personal impact on you. (See Luke 10:25–37; Acts 26:1–32; D&C 50:21–22.)

7. Provide priesthood blessings. Through the ordinances of the priesthood, the power of godliness is manifested. (See D&C 84:20.) Many beautiful messages are revealed and many blessings are received through the ordinances. Ponder their meaning and communicate the wonder of the insights they inspire. Encourage your children to ask for priesthood blessings. (See 3 Ne. 20:2–9; D&C 124:40–41.)

9. Show that we esteem the truths to be of great worth by pondering them and applying them to all facets of our lives. This is essentially the same as the pondering and applying steps under "search diligently," but it needs to be repeated here because the emphasis is different. We do indeed need to ponder

and apply scriptural truths in order to show the Lord that we esteem what he gives us. Again, parents can do much to help their children learn to do these things. Maybe the family needs to mention the problem in family prayer. Maybe it needs to be a subject of family home evening. Children should be encouraged to ponder the situation, and pray for solutions, while they're at school or doing chores or playing with friends. Parents can think and pray about it while at work or doing work around the house or during a daily commute.

10. Show that we esteem the truths to be of great worth by recording what we learn. In our family, when the Lord gives us a great jewel of insight or understanding, we write it down. Either I assign someone to write it in a notebook or on the computer, or I dictate it. But don't just write things down and forget them. Be sure to review from time to time the things you have recorded.

11. Show that we esteem the truths to be of great worth by memorizing scriptures. We've had a lot of fun memorizing in our family. When we find a passage we really love, I say, "Shall we memorize that? Let's all have it memorized by next Sunday, okay?" Now we have a number of scriptures we have all memorized, and when the children are called on to give a talk, they already have a store of the Lord's word in their memories.

12. Show that we esteem the truths to be of great worth by sharing what we're learning with others. When the Lord teaches us a truth, we try to share it with others to show him that we value his gift. When he sees that we'll share what he teaches us, he will often give more because he knows he can trust us to teach and testify to others. Families can share with each other during scripture reading time—and with friends, neighbors, and extended family at other times as well.

As I said earlier, this process is simple. A child can do every one of these things. And once he learns how, he will then begin to follow this pattern in his own reading, and he'll begin to more frequently hear the voice of the Lord giving instruction to him.

I testify again that one of the primary purposes of the scriptures is to help us learn to hear the voice of the Lord. What a blessing to our children if we will help them in this process! If we will let this be one of the major goals of our family scripture reading, we will reap great rewards—and our children will be blessed every day of their lives.

"Why We Love the Scriptures"— One Family's Testimony

We have shared a number of encouraging success stories and testimonies in this book. Each one gives yet another witness of the blessings that come from family scripture study. Here is one final story as we conclude:

> We knew for years we should be having regular family scripture study. But we have been thrilled and amazed at the blessings that began to come once we decided that we would be absolutely consistent—and followed through.
>
> When we truly became serious about scripture reading, our youngest daughter, Amy, was five years old and in kindergarten. Although she was just learning how to read, she always wanted to read at least one verse. Generally we would give her an easy verse—but still the older children groaned at the mispronunciations and frustrating pace. Finally she began to privately study the "Scripture Reader" Doctrine and Covenants. Amy greatly enjoyed reading the few lines of text and looking at the pictures, and she would come into our bedroom almost nightly to read her "*Doctor* and Covenants," as she called it.
>
> As she read the "*Doctor* and Covenants," she developed a love for the Prophet Joseph Smith and felt

genuinely hurt when she read about the mean things people did to him. She couldn't imagine anyone not loving the prophet as much as she did. Naturally, her comprehension and reading skills vastly improved as she read her now well-used scripture book. We were amazed at how quickly she caught on and was reading big words like Nauvoo, priesthood, and Melchizedek. She soon did not require help with very many words and became an outstanding reader in her kindergarten class.

Now, as a second grader, she is way ahead of her class in reading. She prizes her leather quad (a hand-me-down from Dad). She is anxious to look up scriptures (with a little help) and read along with the speakers in sacrament meeting. Her testimony is growing without "compulsory means."

The next older daughter, Allison, really surprised us with her dedication to the scriptures. Unbeknown to us, Allison (age eleven) had set a goal for the "Gospel in Action" award to read the scriptures daily for a month. In the summer of 1994 we went backpacking with two other families. Considering Allison's size and age, we thought she could carry her "needed" clothing, sleeping bag, sleeping pad, and maybe a few light things like packages of oatmeal, hot cocoa, and trail mix. The first evening, after supper, we decided to have a little program. Someone asked, "Did anyone remember to bring your scriptures?" Allison said, "I did!" and she ran to get them out of her pack. When she returned with her quad, we were all very surprised—but she was determined to keep her goal of reading the scriptures daily, even while backpacking. We were grateful Allison had remembered to bring her scriptures, and we used them every evening for our programs.

Our oldest child, Brian, is now in high school. In spite of his heavy load of homework, we often "catch him" reading scriptures late at night. It is a great comfort to know that the children look to the scriptures as a source of strength and guidance.

When Brian was a freshman, he resolved to reach the goal of Master Scriptorian in seminary. He constantly carried his scripture cards with him and worked on memorizing the twenty-five scriptures required for the program. He took advantage of the commute to and from school, memorizing scriptures on the bus. He carried his cards with him as he delivered newspapers and memorized as he worked. When the Varsity Scouts went on a horseback riding trip, Brian carried his scripture cards with him on the horse and memorized as they were riding along. As our family watched general conference that October, Brian recognized many of the scriptures the General Authorities were quoting in their talks and recited them along with the speaker. He reached his goal that year and has every year since.

It hasn't been easy. We have to get up at 5:45 A.M. so we can read before Brian leaves for seminary. But it is a nice way to start the day—we're together as a family, we read the Book of Mormon, and we have the blessing of a family prayer before we all go our separate ways for the day. Something important seems missing when we don't start our days this way. We are so grateful for the scriptures and the opportunities they give us to grow as a family.

CHAPTER 18

A CHALLENGE AND
A TESTIMONY

In this book we have shared many ideas and many testimonies about reading the scriptures. Now what ought we to do?

First, if you, as parents, are not consistently having family scripture study, I strongly recommend that you decide now to make regular scripture study a tradition in your family. If you are having regular family study, I recommend that you resolve today to make it an experience that's even better, even more consistent, even more meaningful, even more spiritual.

Next, talk to your family in a spirit of humility, and touch each one spiritually so that they all commit to join you in that new tradition. (Remember the discussion in chapter 16 about how to invite the Spirit into your family meetings.)

Third, make the spiritual sacrifice to invite and maintain the Spirit of the Lord in your family meetings. Be sure to create a spiritual setting that will drive all contention from your scripture reading experience.

If you do these things, I bear testimony to you that you will receive the fruits of the Spirit in your home—namely, peace, joy, harmony, love, kindness, and the other fruits we all so much desire.

Many years ago we had a lot of little boys in our family. When they asked their mom what she wanted for her birthday

218

or Christmas, she always answered the same: "Peace and harmony." One Christmas we gave her some peas and hominy.

I wondered if we would ever see the day when we would have the real thing on a consistent basis, when we would have true peace and harmony. But I bear testimony that it did come, and it came through our practice of having family scripture reading and family prayer. As you persist in this endeavor, you will enjoy the same blessing. You will gradually remove all contention from your home, and the Spirit of the Lord will reside there.

THE TESTIMONY OF PROPHETS

I am so grateful for the Lord's promises as they are given us through his prophets. Here are some most valuable promises given to us through our latter-day prophets:

President Ezra Taft Benson

Now in the authority of the sacred priesthood in me vested, I invoke my blessing upon the Latter-day Saints. . . . I bless you with increased understanding of the Book of Mormon. I promise you that from this moment forward, if we will daily sup from its pages and abide by its precepts, God will pour out upon each child of Zion and the Church a blessing hitherto unknown. (*Ensign*, May 1986, 78.)

Elder Marion G. Romney

I feel certain that if in our homes, parents will read from the Book of Mormon prayerfully and regularly, both by themselves and with their children, the spirit of that great book will come to permeate our homes and all who dwell therein. The spirit of reverence will increase. Mutual respect and consideration for each other will grow. The spirit of contention will depart. Parents will counsel their children in greater love and wisdom. Children will be more responsive and submissive to that counsel. Righteousness will increase. Faith, hope, and charity, the pure love of Christ will abound in our homes and in our lives, bringing in their wake, peace, joy, and happiness. (Conference Report, April 1960, 112–13.)

President Spencer W. Kimball

Our children may learn the lessons of life through the perseverance and personal strength of Nephi; the godliness of the three Nephites; the faith of Abraham; the power of Moses; the deception and perfidy of Ananias; the courage even to death of the unresisting Ammonites; the unassailable faith of the Lamanite mothers transmitted down through their sons, so powerful that it saved Helaman's striplings. . . . One would surely be blind who could not learn to live life properly by such reading. . . .

Scripture study as individuals and as a family is most fundamental to learning the gospel. Daily reading of the scriptures and discussing them together has long been suggested as a powerful tool against ignorance and the temptations of Satan. This practice will produce great happiness and will help family members love the Lord and his goodness. (*Teachings of Spencer W. Kimball*, 132–33, 129.)

President Howard W. Hunter

Scriptures contain the record of the self-revelation of God, and through them God speaks to man. . . . To understand requires more than casual reading or perusal—there must be concentrated study. It is certain that one who studies the scriptures every day accomplishes far more than one who devotes considerable time one day then lets days go by before continuing. . . .

There is nothing more helpful than prayer to open our

understanding of the scriptures. Through prayer we can attune our minds to seek the answers to our searchings. . . . [I]f we will ask, seek, and knock, the Holy Spirit will guide our understanding if we are ready and eager to receive.

Families are greatly blessed when wise fathers and mothers bring their children about them, read from the pages of the scriptural library together, and then discuss freely the beautiful stories and thoughts according to the understanding of all. (*Ensign*, Nov. 1979, 64.)

President Gordon B. Hinckley

I love our scriptures. I love these wonderful volumes, which set forth the word of the Lord . . . for the guidance of our Father's sons and daughters. I love to read the scriptures, and I try to do so consistently and repeatedly. I like to quote from them. . . . For me, the reading of the scriptures is not the pursuit of scholarship. Rather, it is a love affair with the word of the Lord and that of his prophets. They contain so much for each of us. . . .

Through reading the scriptures, we can gain the assurance of the Spirit that that which we read has come of God for the enlightenment, blessing, and joy of his children.

I urge our people everywhere to read the scriptures more—to study all of them together . . . for a harmony of understanding in order to bring their precepts into our lives.

May the Lord bless each of us to feast upon his holy word and to draw from it that strength, that peace, that knowledge "which passeth all understanding" (Philip. 4:7), as he has promised. (*Ensign*, Dec. 1985, 44, 45.)

My Testimony

I add my testimony to that of these great prophets. I declare to you that what they have said is true. I bear witness of the great benefits that come from searching the words of the Lord.

I pray that you will have a righteous influence over every single one of your children and that you may have great joy in seeing them read their scriptures on their own each day. They will come to do this not because you've told them to, but because they have found for themselves the great power in the word of God. They will also have come to love his holy scriptures.

I bear witness that as we search and live by the words of God, in humility and in the spirit of prayer, we will come to hear the voice of the Lord, and we will receive the guidance, peace, revelation, and blessings we so much need in our lives.

I love the Lord's words. As I conclude my testimony and this book, I would like to leave you with twenty-five reasons why that is so. These put in capsule form why the scriptures mean so much to me.

WHY I LOVE THE SCRIPTURES
(25 PERSONAL REASONS)

The Scriptures Give Revelation and Direction

The scriptures have:

1. Given me answers to difficult problems throughout my whole life. They are full of patterns, with answers to today's problems. (D&C 20:9.)
2. Made me sure and steadfast in my course in life. (Hel. 3:29.)
3. Taught me things that no man knew. (1 Cor. 2:10–11; D&C 33:16.)
4. Been the means through which I have prayerfully received more revelation than any other way. (D&C 32:4.)
5. Been an unshakable, unquestionable standard in life for me and for my family. They have provided a common standard upon which my family and I can rely.
6. Been one of the greatest aids of all in nourishing and teaching my family and me. (Moro. 6:4.)
7. Taught me how to return home. (D&C 35:20.)

8. Been instrumental in my own conversion and in the conversion of numerous nonmembers and less active members throughout my life. (2 Ne. 3:23–24; Hel. 15:7–8.)

9. Filled me with light, revelation, and truth. Their truths have frequently come to me as strokes of pure intelligence. (Luke 24:32.)

10. Been one of the greatest single factors in helping me raise up my family to the Lord.

The Scriptures Bring the Fruits of the Spirit

The scriptures have:

11. Cheered me up, lifted my spirits, and given me hope, comfort, and peace.

12. Along with prayer, been the single greatest developer of my faith. (Rom. 10:17; Hel. 5:7–8.)

13. Had the effect of humbling me. (1 Ne. 15:20.) They have continually brought me to a state of repentance. (2 Tim. 3:15–17.) They have strengthened my commitment to God. (Hel. 15:7–8.)

14. Brought words of peace to my soul. They have reached to the depths of my soul. They are true nourishment to my soul. (3 Ne. 11:3.)

15. Brought peace to my family and largely removed contention.

16. Alerted me to and protected me from temptation. They have given me power to resist. (1 Ne. 15:24.)

The Scriptures Are the Words of the Lord

The scriptures have:

17. Taught me to have total, 100-percent confidence in their direction, their absolute direction. They literally mean what they say. (1 Ne. 13:39; Moro. 10:4–5; Moses 7:62.)

18. Given me vision, wisdom beyond my years, and a more profound understanding of life and of God's purposes. They have lifted my sights to an eternal view. (JS-H 1:73–74.)
19. Led me to Christ and to his Father. They have taught me to be like them. (Deut. 17:19; Hel. 3:29.) They have helped me draw "nearer to God." (Introduction to Book of Mormon.) They have led me, as an iron rod, to the love of God—charity.
20. Been to me the words of the Lord. I love the books themselves and feel they should always be handled with the greatest respect.
21. Been a primary means for my hearing the voice of the Lord. The words of the scriptures are the voice of the Lord to me. (Mosiah 5:12; 3 Ne. 11:3; Moro. 8:7; D&C 18:35–36; 68:4; 84:60.)
22. Revealed to me a multitude of hidden truths throughout. So deep is this "well of living water" that I never will be able to uncover them all.
23. Been a perfect witness of God to me. There is no error in any of our modern scripture (which includes the Book of Mormon).
24. Been a way of rekindling my premortal memory. They speak with a familiar voice to me, as a voice through the veil.
25. Given me the power to avoid deception and combat falsehoods. They have within them the words of pure truth, setting at naught all the subtle teachings, half-truths, false doctrines, and worldly teachings of men and the devil. (2 Ne. 3:12; Hel. 3:29.)

INDEX

225